INTO A
TIMELESS
REALM

Books by Michael J. Roads

The Worlds Beyond Quartet
Talking With Nature
Journey Into Nature
Journey Into Oneness
Into a Timeless Realm

Simple Is Powerful
The Natural Magic of Mulch (Australia only)

INTO A TIMELESS REALM

Michael J. Roads

H J KRAMER
TIBURON, CALIFORNIA

H J Kramer Inc
P.O. Box 1082
Tiburon, CA 94920

Editor: Nancy Grimley Carleton
Editorial Assistant: Claudette Charbonneau
Cover Art: Michael Nicholas
Cover Design: Jim Marin/Marin Graphic Services
Composition: Classic Typography
Book Production: Schuettge and Carleton
Manufactured in the United States of America.
10 9 8 7 6 5 4 3 2 1

Library of Congress Cataloging-in-Publication Data

Roads, Michael J.
    Into a timeless realm : a metaphysical adventure / by
Michael J. Roads.
        p.   cm.
    ISBN 0-915811-66-9 (alk. paper)
    1. Roads, Michael J.   2. Spiritual biography—Australia.
3. Evolution—Miscellanea.   4. Nature—Religious aspects.
5. Spiritual life.   I. Title.
BL73.R6A3   1996
291.4'092—dc20
[B]   95-21211
                                                          CIP

*To Treenie, my wife and partner
in the Fairy Ring.*

To Our Readers

The books we publish
are our contribution to an
emerging world based on cooperation
rather than on competition, on affirmation
of the human spirit rather than on self-doubt,
and on the certainty that all humanity is
connected. Our goal is to touch as many
lives as possible with a message
of hope for a better world.

Hal and Linda Kramer, Publishers

Contents

Acknowledgments

As always, I am indebted to my wife, Treenie. When I finished the manuscript of this book, I gave it to her to read. "Tell me if my readers will think me completely over the top," I asked her.

She read it and came to me. "My dear, now is the timing for such truth. I'm sure that all the people who are ready will easily embrace it."

What can I say? As always, she is an unfailing support. Thank you, my darling.

Once again, I have the support of my publishers, Hal and Linda Kramer. I would like to extend my sincere thanks to them, and also to all their staff who are involved in helping bring this book to you.

Editors are a part of the writing process for all authors. It is usually their lot to deal with rather more worldly subjects than mine, but Nancy Grimley Carleton was once again extremely sensitive and accommodating. Thank you, Nancy.

Once again I am fortunate enough to have a close friend who did the cover art. To Michael Nicholas, one of the

Acknowledgments

very best artists in Australia, thank you for your stunning and graphic vision. It's not many who can capture and paint another person's experience.

I also wish to acknowledge my gratitude to the many Beings of other dimensional realities who have helped me. Written or even verbal thanks only have meaning if they express a true appreciation. My appreciation is expressed by living and sharing the Truth of a Greater Reality.

Introduction

I have detailed my unfolding metaphysical development in three of my previous books, *Talking With Nature,* *Journey Into Nature,* and *Journey Into Oneness.* The events in this book took place a few years preceding those three books. Together, the four books record the mystical events I experienced during an intense nine-year period. What I have written here happened at a time when I lacked the courage to go public. I was afraid of ridicule, afraid of my own inner conflict, and afraid of the strange mystical Reality that was overwhelming me. Beyond all that, there was the matter of timing. This was not a timing that I was to decide, or determine, but a timing of both a physical and metaphysical unfolding. What happened was so extraordinary, so utterly unaccountable, that I could *not* have written this book one day earlier than the day I began it. While this book stands clearly in its own right, it is also an essential prequel to the other three books.

During a particularly difficult period of turmoil and inner conflict in my life, I was suddenly propelled into a startling mystical experience. The manner in which it happened was certainly not harsh, yet it was uninvited and unexpected. This experience totally annihilated my belief that reality is based on the fixed and defined principles of a physical law.

Without a doubt, the prime mover in my mystical encounter was my overwhelming urge to know who I Am. I was just beginning to realize that the more I struggled to learn this universal Truth, the more resistance I seemed to create. The true story I have documented here came at one of my peaks of inner growth and change. Although change and growth were exactly what I wanted, I was never able to reconcile them with the inner hurt and emotional pain that always accompanied them. Like most people, I strenuously resisted my own growth. Such inner conflict inevitably increases and prolongs the trauma!

Much of my emotional confusion was caused by discovering aspects of myself that for a long time had been submerged in my psyche. To the world, I presented myself as a practical man, very down-to-earth, strong, and capable, with just a touch of aggression. I really thought this was me. Then I made a disturbing inner discovery. At the time of the events recounted in this book, I had just learned that this was my act, the mask I wore.

With the act of a lifetime harshly stripped away, I felt vulnerable and exposed. I was shocked to discover my demoralizing self-doubt, to find that my self-esteem was almost nil. This, combined with a potent inner longing to know who I Am, was undoubtedly the pivotal factor in bringing about my metaphysical adventure.

I knew that something was building up when I had the

dream that revealed my subconscious self-deceit. It was a simple enough dream, but it hit me hard. I dreamt that while living in my house, I discovered the door to a room I had never before seen or known about. I opened the door and went in. The room was old, yet fine and grand, but it had obviously been unused for a very long time. There were various pieces of elegant furniture, and my eyes were drawn to a huge antique cupboard on the far side of the room. I went over to it and opened the doors. Inside were several shelves of beautiful porcelain vases and delicate bone china crockery, all stacked away very neatly. Then, a slight movement at the bottom of the cupboard caught my eye. I knelt down to see what it was, and I was shocked to see a tiny figure trying to conceal itself in the gloom.

As I stared, I saw that a small, gnomelike creature was huddled in the shadows in the depths of the cupboard, and I felt an instant, and unexpected, surge of love for this diminutive Being. Very gently, I tried to scoop it up into my arms, but it twisted away from me, backing into the gloom.

"Come out into the light where I can see you," I asked, but it only shrank farther away from me.

Finally, with much coaxing, I enticed it to the door of the cupboard, where I could see it more clearly. I gasped. A tiny human male, he was about two feet tall, with thin, sticklike limbs and a withered body. Not gnomelike at all, he was a stunted, shrunken, dwarfed, human manikin. I was confused, because, unaccountably, I felt a very strong emotional attachment to the manikin, with inexplicable feelings of love for him surging through me.

Introduction

"Who are you?" I asked.

He looked at me shyly. "Don't you know?"

"Of course I don't. How could I?"

"I am your self-love," he replied.

I woke up crying, an outburst of gut-wrenching tears shaking my whole body as I cried from the very depths of my Being. I could no longer evade my truth. I had long ago buried my self-love in some deep, inaccessible part of me, replacing it with an unrealized fabrication of self-deceit. In that moment of recognition, I saw so clearly how I was unknowingly living a lie.

Eventually, when my exhausted emotions had stabilized, I made a silent pledge to the manikin. Never again would I ignore my self-love. Very clearly, I knew that when I finally "fell in Love with Self," I would know who I Am. With aware deliberation, I placed the manikin in my heart. I did not know, then, that there would be many more years of emotional hurt, intense physical pain, confusion, deep inner confrontations, and many metaphysical challenges, before this Awakening, this "falling in Love with Self," would take place.

Owing to my total acceptance of the dream, and my pledge to nurture and nourish my self-love, the metaphysical aspect of Self that had been released became my catalyst, propelling me into a metaphysical Reality beyond my wildest dreams.

After nearly forty years of relating to myself basically as a very physical person, I found it challenging and alarming to find myself facing an unknown, unrealized, metaphysical aspect of Self. I was to learn that while my practical, logical self was strong, my metaphysical Self was volcanic in its power. I learned that the reality that most of us accept as real and normal is no more than a mutually accepted illusion, mass self-deceit, or, as it is more generally known, consensus reality. Just as I had to remove the masks that hid my greater Self from me, each one of us, individually, has to go through his or her own process of unmasking. Beyond this, humanity as a Whole has to remove the suffocating masks that hide us—a race of intelligent Beings—from our Greater metaphysical Reality.

This book documents a major step along the way as I made the journey from a normal. mundane, limited reality, to the enlightened and magnificent Reality that is the birthright of every Being.

1

A Shift in Reality

With our physical ears,
we hear the echoes,
but an open heart may hear
the full, metaphysical Song of Life.

The sigh that escaped my lips as I awoke was echoed and magnified by the wind as it prowled around our house. I glanced at the illuminated dial at our bedside: two o'clock in the morning and pitch-dark. For long moments, the remnants of an incredible dream surged into my mind, then rapidly began to recede. Feeling that the dream was important, I strained to remember, but as I did so, it faded into nothing.

I yawned and stretched, catching my breath as a sharp stab of pain lanced through my ankle. Despite all this nocturnal activity, Treenie, my wife, remained deeply asleep, so I lay back with a wry smile, remembering the events that led up to my present sorry state.

For about two weeks, I had been receiving strong inner promptings to slow down my hectic pace in life. My intuition had been working overtime trying to tell me that I needed to spend some time in meditative silence. I had a strong feeling that it was important to turn my energies inward, and I kept meaning to—tomorrow!

I was rather apprehensive about turning within. Each

time I followed my inner urgings to do this, I would go through a process of inner growth that would invariably leave me traumatized. Although I had to concede that each episode was another step up the ladder of Self-realization, this ladder was fraught with pain and suffering. So for the last couple of weeks I had procrastinated, even though I knew that whatever I was avoiding would eventually catch up with me—and, most likely, with a vengeance.

I sighed heavily again, hoping I would wake Treenie without meaning to wake her! She didn't even stir, so I continued my musing.

Whatever it was that wanted me to slow down and tune in had caught up with me yesterday. I had been running along our garden path, happily charging into my next diversion from any inner contemplation, when my right foot came down on the outer edge of the concrete path. As my unsupported foot rolled over, my ankle popped out of joint with an explosion of pain.

I was in agony. This ankle was already chronically weakened by a number of previous sprains, and the joint now had a permanent gap. At the moment of dislocation, the pain was so intense that I was never sure whether to faint or vomit. However, it invariably took me off my feet to a horizontal position, away from all hurry and haste, providing the opportunity for many hours of inner contemplation. I sighed again. What a stupid way to live, responding only to the stimulus of pain and suffering.

With sudden clarity, the dream surged powerfully into my mind. It remained disjointed, yet I had the impression of some strange, exotic place, where an impossible reality promoted equally impossible experiences. Feeling the need to talk, I was about to wake Treenie deliberately, when my normal, everyday reality came to an abrupt and shocking end.

Everything in our bedroom seemed to move into a slow time—Treenie's breathing, my movements, even my thoughts. Despite the turmoil of my emotions while held in this state of suspension, I was calm and accepting, as though some other influence controlled me. With no understanding of what was happening, I watched from my physical reality while another me stepped out of my physical body.

In that moment, I was aware of being two completely different aspects of Self, both happening simultaneously. In one reality, I was the normal physical me, wide awake and aware of a painful throb in my damaged ankle. I sat up in bed and, without any thought behind my action, picked up the large writing pad and pen that is always at my bedside. Calmly, I began to write down the events that unfolded in my other reality.

The other me had a body of light, closely resembling my normal, physical self. I did not glow with light, nor was I illuminated, but I was aware of being composed entirely of light. I climbed out of bed, stepping onto an ankle that had never known an injury. Without a backward glance, I went through the open bedroom door and walked out. Moving silently through the house, I passed through the closed backdoor, walking out into a glorious dawn. With a strong wind, it was dark in my physical reality, but in this "otherness" it was calm and light.

The physical me sat in bed writing all this down. I had no recollection of switching on my low-glow bedside lamp in the moonless, pitch-dark night, but it gave me just enough light to see my writing on the paper. Although I was aware of both my physical self and the light-body me, practically all my focus, attention, and awareness were with my light-body self. Not for a second did I have a thought about how odd this was, nor what I could do to escape this strange, mystical occurrence. Everything about my physical reality was overwhelmed by a supernatural, calm acceptance. I had one physical function only, and that was to record the experiences of my light-body self.

Undisturbed, Treenie slept on.

I walk by taking normal footsteps, yet there is no feeling of weight in my body. I know that it should be dark by any measure of normality, but equally, everything that is normal has ended. The brighter than possible rays of gold that haze across the sky like the billowing of a gigantic wisp of gauze, feel acceptable and normal. I know that I am going down to the river, but I have no idea why. Walking feather light across the field toward the distant waterway, I am aware that every blade of grass is alive and vital within both itself and the Whole. Each blade of grass is a unit within itself, yet also with the plant from which it grows, and with the pasture as a Whole. I perceive that Nature is really a creative living principle, forever demonstrating the One in All, the All in One.

As I realize this, I become aware of the dew beading the blades of grass. Each separate drop is a tiny reservoir of energy. In some mystical way, I see each drop magnified, physically reflecting the gold in the sky, yet in some inner impression I see all the water of Earth, alive and aware.

Continuing across the field, I feel an inner exuberance as my awareness expands and stretches, breaking free from its long, restrictive confinement. Silence is so powerful that it becomes a shout, startling me as I feel a surge and rush of inner hearing. Now, I can hear the Song of the grass, a sound of surprising power, yet exquisitely delicate. Each drop of dew is a vibrating echo, adding to the harmonic of the grass. I know, without knowing how I know, that dewdrops are a harmonic amplifier of energy for each plant on which they collect.

Each footstep I take becomes a lesson. Every tiny pebble underfoot has its story to tell, and I can hear. I listen to the microscopic organisms in the soil as they follow their own movement in the orchestration of Earth life, and I listen to the dawn chorus of the birds. To listen physically to the local birds welcoming a new day is always a joy, but to inner-hear is joy magnified beyond measure. My body of light thrills and resonates to the quality of sound, while my inner Being dances and pirouettes to Nature's Song. And I know that this radiant, inaudible Silence is another submerged, unrealized truth in our physical reality. With our physical ears, we hear the echoes, but an open heart may hear the full, metaphysical Song of Life.

I reach the riverbank, and, without warning, I am engulfed in timelessness. I am abruptly held in the grip of some timeless power. In suspension, transfixed, I am unable to move, or even breathe. My first, immediate flutters of fear vanish, as I meekly surrender to some vast, unimaginable power. All time and all life within this strange Reality are held in this magical suspension. Even the river is unmoving, each ripple held by the thrall of some immortal will. Beyond my vision, I am aware that the river is flowing normally to a certain point within my vicinity; then, it becomes unmoving. There is no backup of water, no sign of anything abnormal. Impossibly, at some place farther downriver, the water continues flowing toward the sea.

Standing immobile, I watch as the sky bursts into flaming color. Burnt orange, resplendent red, and molten gold mix and merge, to be pulled to earth as the river catches and reflects this riot of color. Blazing, burnished color consumes everything in this riotous display of heaven's furnace. Across the river, the reeds are golden red, the same fiery color embracing the river, the trees, me, and, incredibly, a heron that is standing transfixed in the shallows, its beak holding an immobile fish. Heron and fish are sculptured from a forge of living fire. I can perceive and identify images of reality far beyond the range of my eyes, yet even my perception is overwhelmed and awed by this conflagration of magical color.

Although my fear has vanished, for long moments my mind rages against the sheer impossibility of this unworldly scene. Then, deep inside my psyche, I clearly feel something snap. Immediately, the heron leaps into the air, flying with a harsh croak past the curve of the river, while the water is now chuckling and gurgling quietly as it flows swiftly over the stony bed. The riot of color fades swiftly, until once again the sky is a soft, billowing gold over a backdrop of blue. The reeds are again a familiar dark green fringe bordering the crystal-clear water.

I release my long-held breath in a gentle sigh. I know now that breathing in my light body is no more than the continuation of a physical necessity. Light is both my breath and my nourishment. Momentarily, I wonder what has snapped within me, but I am not concerned. An inner wisdom suggests that it is the breaking of a link, overstretched and weakened as I strained against the restricting chains of disbelief and a purely physical reality.

A movement catches my eye, and I turn around to see that Treenie is standing nearby.

I gasp. "What are you doing here?"

"Trying to decide if I am in your dream, or if you are in mine," she says, smiling.

"Did you get frozen in time just now? How did you get here?" The questions tumble out of me.

"Michael, hold on a minute. I only know that I'm asleep, dreaming. Equally, it appears that I'm involved in something with you, but I only arrived here the moment you saw me."

"But I'm not asleep," I protest. "I'm awake. My physical self is sitting in bed writing this down as it happens, while the metaphysical me is here, in this light body." I waggle my hands in her face. "So, how can you be here if you are asleep?"

Treenie gives me a look of exasperation. "Why don't you face the obvious? I *am* here, aware and conscious. It's my body that is asleep. So I suggest you get on with it."

Perplexed, I stare at her. "What are you talking about? Get on with what?"

"Get on with whatever it is you came here to do."

"I don't know why I'm here," I say in bewilderment. "This whole thing began without any prompting from me. I haven't a clue what's going on." I smile at her. "But I'm really glad that you're here."

Stepping closer, I reach out to embrace her, but somehow we seem to be out of phase. I'm disconcerted to find I cannot touch her. As my arms encircle her, we seem to occupy slightly different realities, and we miss. I attempt to kiss her willing lips, but there is no contact.

I shrug. "It seems there is a difference between your dream state and my metaphysical reality, but at least I can see you and hear you. I'll happily settle for that."

A faint buzzing vibration catches my attention. It comes from a bit farther downriver, and for a moment, I wonder if it is the orchestrated noise of cicadas. This sound, however, is much deeper and unnaturally low, conveying far more emphasis with its vibration than its sound.

"What's that strange buzzing?" Treenie asks.

"I don't know, but it sure is intense."

Dismissing the cicada theory, yet curious, I continue my walk downriver to investigate, accompanied by Treenie.

As I skirt around a dense thicket of tall bamboo, the path

takes me away from the river. Light, dancing through the dark green bamboo, bounces from cane to cane with an elusive grace. Despite an absence of breeze, the canes stir, whispering in their leafy tops as I pass. I feel encouraged, until finally, passing beneath some river pines, we emerge again on the riverbank.

Much closer now to the weird buzzing sound, I tingle with the intensity of its vibration. A feeling not unlike pins and needles sweeps through me, while the buzzing seems to be right inside my head. Although I am mildly disturbed, I am not at all distressed.

"Do you get a pins-and-needles feeling?" I ask.

Treenie nods. "It's so agitating, it's difficult to be here." She points, her eyes wide with wonder. "But look at the river."

I gaze in awe at the river. It seems as though a vast pressure is pushing down onto the water's surface, like some intangible but gigantic bubble. I am aware of a spherical shape, maybe one hundred feet or so in diameter, that is filled with such an intensity of sound that even the air is distorted and blurred. The surface of the river is bulging downward from the pressure, while all the reeds and riverside vegetation are flattened. Yet, in all this, not so much as a breath of wind stirs the air. All is unnaturally calm and eerily motionless.

I flinch, shocked, as without warning the vast sphere of pressure suddenly appears to consume the river where it flows into the affected area. The water just disappears, leaving the riverbed open and bare. Gradually now, the huge buzzing sphere becomes opaque, as though filled with water, and I can see pictures forming and dissolving within its interior.

Even for my unnaturally calm light-body self, the shock is too much. Trying to grab Treenie, I want to turn and run. I want to get us as far away from this crazy, impossible reality as I can. But even as I gather myself in an attempt to sprint away from the river, time and motion are again abruptly suspended.

Despite my fear, I can do nothing. I cannot even collapse on the bank. Held by some power beyond my own will, I am compelled to face the vast sphere of unknown cosmic forces—and watch. And again, under this other influence, I am now calm and tranquil, compelled to accept this bizarre reality without any disturbance.

I'm not sure what has happened to Treenie. I cannot see her, and I am unable to call out to her. I don't know whether she is near me, and held under the same compulsion, or if her slightly different phase of reality allows her a greater freedom. I only hope that she is okay.

How long I crouch in a position to run, I will never know. Time is static, irrelevant, yet it seems that ages pass while I stare at the unformed, continually dissolving pictures. Try as I might, I cannot make any sense of the fleeting images. Just as I think there might be some meaning within a sequence, it goes wild and random. The harder I try to understand, the more confused I become.

Suddenly, to my delight, I hear Treenie's voice.

"Relax, Michael, just relax. Let it be."

Simply knowing that she is still with me is an enormous relief. I realize that she has projected her thoughts to me, so I attempt to do the same. "Are you okay?" I ask her.

"I'm fine, but like you, I'm not going anywhere."

"Aren't you frightened?"

"Why should I be? I've had far worse dreams than this."

"What do you mean, dreams? I keep telling you that this isn't a dream. This is a metaphysical reality that is happening in a wide-awake state of consciousness."

"It may well be for you, but for me it lacks real clarity. I get moments when everything goes vague."

"It's the opposite for me. I don't recall ever experiencing anything as clearly and sharply defined as this. There is more clarity in my sight, hearing, and perception than is possible in a physical reality. Tell me, are you looking at a sphere filled with a mass of confused images?"

"Yes, I am. But my intuition tells me that it is confused because you are, so just relax and let it be."

"But surely I need to understand what's happening."

"Most probably, yes, but you can't force it. Relax."

Her words make a lot of sense, so I quit attempting to understand, feeling an inner relaxation as I simply watch, without any attempt at comprehension. More than anything, I am pleased that Treenie is still with me.

2
The Sphere of Images

*Our deep despairs are also
our unrealized triumphs,
for it is then that the fabric
of our potential wings strengthen
beneath the cocoon of our self-deception.
From our despair, Truth emerges.*

The moment I relax and quit trying, my confusion ends. The pictures are now clear and precise, and without any effort, my attention becomes powerfully focused. I can now understand what was previously a confused jumble of nonsense. Treenie was right—attempting to force understanding had been counterproductive.

Within the translucent sphere of pressure, I can see moving, holographic images of an unbelievably ancient Earth. With the images, a silent, inner commentary explains some of what I see. This commentary is not spoken, but enfolds into my consciousness in what feels like little waves and ripples of directed knowing.

Without any attempt at speaking and forming words in my immobile state, I project my thoughts to Treenie.

"Can you see what I am seeing?"

"I rather think so," comes her clear reply.

"Are you getting an inner commentary with it?"

"If you mean an inner understanding that seems to accompany it, yes. But it leaves my questions unanswered."

"I'm delighted that you're with me," I tell her.

"I'm very glad to be with you."

Astonished, I see Beings of energy that have form but no physical matter as they drift in small groups over a very strange Earth. Bright to the point of whiteness, the sun creates an atmosphere of illuminated brilliance. Vegetation exists, but even this is lacking in substance. I learn that the ethereal Beings are in an early stage of their evolution, prior to taking on physicality, and they are *human*. Apparently there are many stages to be passed through before the Spirit of humanity is ready to express in dense physical matter.

There are no spoken words, but I am aware of thought and feeling between the Beings as they gracefully make their way across a field of delicate, pale blue vegetation. Occasionally, the Beings pick fronds from plants to ingest for nourishment. They do this by clasping the fronds to the front of their bodies, where they seem to be absorbed quickly. Although most of their nourishment comes from the sun, they are compelled to supplement it. I learn that this is part of their path to physicality. These ethereal Beings have form, but they lack a clear definition. They aren't wispy, or foggy, but undefined. Their thoughts register little more than the mildest curiosity about things around them, suggesting an almost passive nature.

They all appear to be about the same size in slender, five-foot bodies that neither walk nor fly, but are somehow drifting. Their features are indistinct. They don't seem to have a real mouth, nose, eyes, or ears, yet I get the impression that these will eventually appear as they evolve into a more physical reality. Everything about the ethereal Beings has a dreamlike quality, yet I am aware of their attunement with Nature in this preemergent human expression.

I can see no animals, and, apart from the delicate, pale blue fernlike vegetation, no other forms of Nature. Also, I become aware that there are only very few of the ethereal Beings. I get the impression that there is little intellectual development in these Beings, but there is a keen and undoubted intelligence.

Everything fades, the translucent sphere going momentarily blank; then all I can see is black darkness. As I watch, I learn that this phase of the sun is ending, and darkness prevails for a long, long time.

Where the sun is during these long aeons, I have no idea.

"Treenie, did you see the race of ethereal Beings?"

"Yes, I did. They were very beautiful."

"And you got the inner dialogue and insight with it?"

"Yes, but it was sketchy. My intuition tells me that this whole experience is basically for you, and that I'm here as a support—for a while."

"What do you mean for a while? I want you here."

I feel a smile in her thoughts. "This is your reality. I'm only here in a dream state. It all gets a bit vague now and then. Like you often do at home."

My smile is on the inside. "Thanks a lot!"

As the sphere again becomes clear, I see images of a race of Beings who look as though they are unsure whether to be ethereal or physical. Their bodies seem to be a marriage of the ethereal to flesh and bone, resulting in a strange, translucent quality. They are obviously physical, yet they appear opaque and fragile. I can see a thin, lightweight bone structure covered in a substance looking more like firm jelly than the flesh of today. But they are physical. Tall and slender, they walk with fluid ease and a natural, unhuman grace.

"Can you see these zombies?" I call silently.

I feel the reproach in Treenie's reply. "Don't be so flippant. It's disrespectful. Did you ever see such natural and graceful elegance?"

As I watch, I become aware of a relationship with Nature quite unlike anything of today. I learn that some of these Beings—both male and female—by singing certain Songs of attunement and power are able to cause a particular species of tree to take on the shape of the Singer's will. In this way, they grow their homes. I watch a small group of these gifted Beings as they travel from one village to another, singing to the prepared and selected immature young trees.

It is odd, for although I am aware of both males and females, I cannot see any clear difference between the sexes. None of them wear any clothing, so if they have any genitals they must be held within their bodies.

"They are not as sexy as you," I project playfully.

There are no words, but I am hit by an avalanche of strong, very Treenie-like disapproval. I inner-chuckle.

The Nature I see here is dominated by trees—not primitive, prehistoric trees, but species of leaf and flower, and incredible diversity. Just as these Beings can sing a tree into growing into a large, hut-sized bulbous shape for the people to live in, they are also able to sing other trees into growing limbs vaguely shaped as chairs, tables, and other unrecognizable items that may be furniture. The trees they inhabit are always long-lived and alive. If a tree dies, the people living in it move out.

"Just imagine being able to sing your furniture into shape and form," I project.

"Maybe it's a long dormant possibility even for us."

"I think we have a lot of conflict and confusion to deal with first. I get the feeling that the purpose and clarity of these people are undiluted by personal problems or everyday affairs," I say.

"I don't think these people have any such thing as personal problems," Treenie replies.

I am puzzled by her remark, but my attention is on the sphere. I am able to empathize with the respect these people feel for each other and for Nature. Their whole life is a commitment to Nature. Everything they wear, everything they eat and need, comes from their almost symbiotic relationship with the trees. And these, too, are *human* Beings. The silent inner commentary gives no indication of time values for what I am seeing. I get the feeling that rather than predating our present time, what I am seeing coexists with us in a different frame of an infinite Reality. I am unclear about this. Although our linear time structure is based on a concept of beginnings and endings, infinity must surely be based in a greater holistic Reality of timelessness.

As scene after scene unfolds, I become more relaxed

within myself—as opposed to compelled calmness—and I am more able to empathize with these Beings. They surprise me, for they are without desire, without needs, even without real joy or laughter. There is a bliss in them, in the way they are, but no enthusiasm or passion. I perceive that their more ethereal, less physical reality reflects an overall lack of individual drive or desire to achieve.

It occurs to me what Treenie meant by her last remark.

"You mean that these people have a complete lack of any individuality, don't you?" I ask her. "How incongruous, that collectively they seem to have so much, and yet at the same time to have so little personally."

She is silent for some moments. "Yes, I noticed their lack of individuality at once. At least they don't have our modern day hang-ups," she reflects. "But I agree, it seems such an idyllic way to live, in harmony with Nature, yet many of our present qualities are missing."

"What a different perspective it offers," I muse. "No matter how misunderstood or misguided our personal powers may be, within our passion and drive to challenge, to struggle against the odds, and to overcome, we hold the potential as individuals to experience Self as One with the All. To do this, I suspect that we need all the qualities we presently have."

"Perhaps these people also experience themselves as One with the All," Treenie suggests.

"As a human collective maybe, but it's impossible as individuals without individuality. Maybe even Oneness has many levels of human expression."

I feel admiration and love for the ethereal/physical people

that I am witnessing, and I am made aware that their consciousness is with humanity today. All the qualities that they have brought into creation reside within our present soul awareness.

With this realization, the sphere momentarily goes blank. Once again it is opaque, and I can only wonder at what this means. Is this a past civilization that has ended? Somehow, I think not.

Gradually, the sphere again takes on new life and vitality. The semi-physical Beings and the gentle touch of Nature have gone. I am now looking at a scene dominated by rocks and desert, with oceans of distant grass waving in the breeze. I silently wonder if this is the same place at another time. As I ponder this, I get the feeling that I am seeing yet another frame in an infinite Reality, but I am sure that these frames are linked.

"This is different!" I project to Treenie.

No reply.

Another race of Beings throngs the area as they work with a casual ease. I learn that these are also a peaceful race, but whereas the earlier Beings had worked with Nature and the trees, these people work with minerals and water. In a way that I cannot comprehend, they use water to mine the land, taking it deep into the ground. From the commentary, I learn that some of our vast, subterranean caves of today are not the random chance of aeons of oceans and rivers cutting them out as we believe, but the deliberate act of another *human* race, unrecorded in our history.

I learn that each of the eras I am watching predates our

prehistoric period by a vast span of time as we measure it. Long, long, before the beginnings of our prehistoric period, there were intelligent human Beings evolving and flourishing on our planet Earth. I am confused, for it seems certain that the frames of reality I am witnessing interlink the history of Earth into a vast, immeasurable, overall frame of timelessness. The commentary, however, gives me no clarity on this apparent paradox.

"Treenie, are you still with me?"

"Yes, my darling."

"Do you realize that everything we are seeing of the past is somehow held in the present?"

"Yes. But I'm not sure that we need attempt to understand it. Better to go with the flow of it."

I inner-smile my agreement.

The Beings in the image are short, sturdy, and fully physical. However, in a similar way to both the earlier ethereal and semi-physical races, all the mature adults conform in size, weight, and even looks. Again, the unmistakable imprint of personal individuality is absent. Whereas the semi-physical Beings had a milky white translucency and were hairless, these people are black skinned with a definite tan pigmentation, and have black, frizzy hair. Perhaps that is because the semi-physical people lived under a sky of almost permanent cloud, while these mineral and water workers live under an intense sun. Although it defies logic, their sun is far hotter and more intense than our sun of today.

The ability of these Beings with minerals is all but supernatural. I watch as a molten, liquid mineral is propelled under tremendous pressure from a spout, where it points toward the sky. As the jet of molten liquid shoots in a thin, continuous stream up into the air, it is met at a calculated angle by an equal jet of water. Clouds of steam burst forth as the two liquids meet, but as they fall to Earth, the mineral is now formed into flat, paper-thin platelets. For some unfathomable reason, the platelets don't appear to quite touch the Earth, drifting just above the ground in heaps, as though they were large silver snowflakes. All that remains of the water is a fine misty spray, for most of it is converted into steam on contact with the molten mineral.

As before, everything and everybody conforms to a certain rhythm and style. The dynamic of our present individuality is again missing.

"The phenomenon persists," I say. "Even in these very human-looking people, there is not real individuality."

"I agree. It's even more apparent in these people," Treenie replies. "Only when you witness its absence do you realize how tangible and potent the power of human individuality really is. And it's odd that there are no children or aged people. How is that possible?"

"Beats me."

I gaze at a technology that is both beyond and before anything in our present time—not so much better, but based on totally different principles. Whereas I suspect that force is the dominating factor in today's technology, this pre-prehistoric human race uses a natural harmonic. In a completely different way from the earlier race, these people also combine with Nature to draw forth the things they need for their growth and survival. And yet, these people also seem to be without any real needs or desires.

"I bet if I asked these people why they do what they do, they would not even comprehend the question," I say.

"Yes. They seem to do what they do simply because this is what they do. It's strange that their whole energy conveys this lack of a defined purpose so clearly. Equally, I don't think that they would understand the concept of survival."

Even as we briefly comment on what we see, the scene continues to unfold. Because of the intense heat, the dwellings of these Beings are deep underground, carved by water with a superb accuracy. This is not a matter of simply gauging out the rock with pressurized water, and then living in what results. Far from it. They *know* the structure, nature, and formation of solid rock to a degree that far exceeds our present understanding of the structure of a manufactured brick! When the water is "introduced" into rock, it tunnels and excavates to the exact size and dimensions that have been calculated and projected. This may be a simple construct, or one of amazing complexity. To perform this incredible feat, a group of the Beings enters a trancelike state, becoming the directive nexus in the merging consciousness of humans, rock, and water.

"I could make a fortune if I could learn how to control water like that."

"Michael! Don't be so frivolous."

Some of the underground caverns are of such immense proportions that they can house a whole city of people. Within this, carved by the architectural expertise of humans

23

and water, are many smaller structures that house small groups. And, within all this, the breathtaking flair of curves, archways, and sweeping grace must surely have been given birth again in our cathedrals of today.

Once more, the sphere goes blank for a few moments, and then I witness an age of wind gripping our planet, lasting for what seems an eternity. Unending wind of a ferocity that scours and levels mountains. I witness what appears as the ending of this age, and then, the birth of new life.

I am deeply puzzled by this. More powerfully than ever, I get a sense of timelessness, yet what I am seeing suggests the end of an Age.

I share my speculation with Treenie. "How can you have timelessness alongside beginnings and endings?" I ask. "It just isn't possible, surely."

"I think I know what you mean, but perhaps you are too preoccupied with time and timelessness. And who knows? Conceivably it may be possible. It occurs to me that perhaps both realities are happening. Perhaps we are witnessing different root races in the development of humanity that belong in our far distant linear past, yet, at the same time, are also an ongoing part of human development in other frames of a greater infinite Reality."

"Talk about pondering the imponderable! I think I'll call it Mystery, and leave it alone," I say, watching the sphere as it continues to change.

Again, in an era prior to our prehistoric age, another race of *humanity* is to be seen. This time, the sun is weak, the climate cold. I cannot see any oceans, but rivers of a great width are as prolific on the land as are the lines on a human hand. What seems odd is that most of the rivers run in uneven parallels to one another, seldom crossing or intersecting. Many of the rivers are of solid ice, while the others flow with a slow, sluggish power.

I now watch a nomadic race of people as they wander the Earth. Of average height, their skin is a yellowish color, their hair black and very long. They are slender, yet the long, stringy ropes of muscle on their arms and legs give evidence to immense stamina. These people are very well adapted to their lifestyle. Although their limbs are bare, their bodies are well wrapped, but I am certain that they are physically male and female in the manner of our present human race. Despite clothing, the sexual differences are as obvious as they are today. Also, for the first time I can see young children, adolescents, and the elderly.

"Happy now?" I ask. "The whole family is here. You know, it seems to suggest that those previous people were somehow assimilating into human physicality without being sexual, or reproducing in that way."

"Hmmm, you could be right. I don't know how that's possible but it makes sense. Maybe they have to develop sexuality before individuality can come into expression. I wouldn't say this race has a highly developed individuality, but it is definitely evident," Treenie replies.

The vegetation is mostly coarse grass and scrub, while the seemingly endless vast plains between the rivers writhe beneath the touch of a ceaseless wind that scours the land. Animals are visible everywhere, but I can see no birds. Defying any logic, all the animals I can see are of a single species, like a very large cavy, or guinea pig, approximately

25

the same size as the present-day tailless capybaras that live by the rivers of tropical South America.

These tame and docile animals are used to carry packs, to pull sleds, and to feed and clothe the people. Even the wild cavylike animals are without any fear, calmly ignoring the wandering nomads as they browse on the plains grass and scrub. Without the animals, the nomads could not exist. The nomads' attitude toward their own animals is almost sacred in its concern and attention. Despite the fact that the animals do all the pulling and heavy carrying, they are slavishly catered to by the wanderers. I watch in astonishment as an animal is taken for food. Once separated from the others, two of the men wash it in what is clearly a ritual of chant and prayer. Next, two women approach the animal, and the men depart. Sitting next to the calm creature, they croon to it, sweet and low. Affected by their crooning, I feel that a door is opening into some other dimension, such is the power and intensity it evokes. Maybe it does, for suddenly the animal rolls over, dead.

I am affected by what I see—affected by the power of the connection between the women and the animal. This is not a betrayal, but a true exchange of energy.

There is emotion in my words as I convey this to Treenie. "They harmonize with Nature and the animals so that all needs are met in perfect synchronicity. Today, we exploit for profit, with little real concern for the animals."

"Maybe, but this sort of skill is lost to us."

Mentally shrugging my agreement with her, I learn that the animals willingly surrender their life for the people, as they are sung back to spirit. Like the previous races, these people also express a deep reverence for Nature.

Again, the change.

No wind to purge the land this time, but ice. Unrelenting, rock-shattering glaciers of ice.

For the first time I am grateful that I cannot run or feel real fear. In my normal reality, I would desperately run from the scene that unfolds before me. I see a city of clay, yet it is built on a prodigious scale. I get the impression that I am watching something from a horror film, for the race of soldiers walking in file through the city leaves me chilled and frightened. Each man is about twelve feet tall, with a corresponding width to his shoulders and depth of chest. They are giants—and they, too, are *human*. I feel an inner shudder pass through me. The brutality of the soldiers is so palpable that I try to shrink into invisibility.

Shocked, I project my thoughts to Treenie. "My God! What do you think of this?"

Silence.

"Treeeeenieee! Can you hear me?"

Silence.

The buildings that line the streets are so large that even the most squalid are built to the proportions of our churches and museums. I realize that this is a slum area, for no matter how foreign it appears, the signs of poverty are universal. Way out in front of the soldiers, people scatter, running for cover and shouting in harsh, guttural voices. Most of these people are smaller in stature, but even so, they are all over nine feet tall. Overwhelming everything is fear—

a fear so powerful that I can feel it emanating from the image that I am compelled to watch.

I learn from the inner commentary that the soldiers wear a type of armor that is made from a metal-like substance, lightweight and flexible. It gleams in the sunlight, yet its reflection is fear. The soldiers all have a dark tan complexion, their features harsh, arrogant, and without any trace of compassion. Suddenly, a large rock comes hurtling from a huge window, striking one of the soldiers in the face. Even as he falls, a projectile like a large flat plate comes spinning from another window, its razor edge nearly severing the neck of another soldier. Without a glance at their fallen comrades, the soldiers rush into the building, each drawing a massive broadsword from a huge flat sheath strapped to his back. Each vast sword is about five feet long and about half that in width. Used as both shield and sword in a dazzling display of power and skill, the soldiers deflect a few more missiles and wade with flashing, bloody blades into the screaming people pouring out of all the neighboring doorways. I sense a feeling of shock, as though such an attack on the soldiers is almost unheard of.

What happens next I will never know, for thankfully, the image blurs and changes, yet it remains with the giants.

Urgently, I try to communicate with Treenie. "Did you see all that? Are you still with me?"

Silence.

I can now see a pastoral scene, reasonably peaceful, yet the domination and control of the many by a few is obvious. A few of the soldier types are overseeing other pale-skinned giants as they work on a farm. Two huge animals, looking vaguely like a cross between a reptile and a horse, are pulling a cleverly designed ploughlike implement through the soil. It rips the soil with ease, while others of the same strange animal combination are being used to fell trees and clear the soil of its natural vegetation.

The trees are no larger than the trees of today, nor the vegetation more abundant. Insects swarm everywhere, far more than is natural or normal today, while animals of a strange warm-blooded reptilian nature seem to be the dominant animal form. Again I see no birds.

All traces of a harmonious relationship with Nature are gone. I learn—with a shock—that the odd reptile/horse combination is a result of genetic manipulation. The animal pulling the plough is huge and very powerful, and it seems to be extremely cunning. I learn that these animals constantly try to kill their handlers, but to little avail. One of the reasons for this extremely aggressive behavior is that they live in constant pain. These animals are created by the giants in laboratories, and such is the divergence from Nature that the creatures pay a price in pain. Pain is their companion from their manipulated birth to their eventual death.

I wish that I could get some comment from Treenie. Is she still with me, or has she woken up? "Treenie, are you with me? Can you see the giants?"

Silence.

Slightly bothered by hearing nothing from Treenie, I watch as scene after scene in the life of the giants gives me an overall picture of their horrendous culture. In a time that far predates our prehistoric era—and yet, somehow continues to coexist with now—humanity is struggling to become human. The cruelty is not limited to the dark soldier race, for the persecuted pale giants deal with one another in a manner of careless brutality. The men treat women appallingly, and they in turn are harsh and intolerant with their children. No children are ever born from an act of love; they are the offspring of the couplings of lust and sexual dominance. Our modern-day animals show a far greater regard for their offspring and family than this depraved race of giants.

I see no evidence of any machines, or indeed of anything that remotely resembles an engine. The metal-like substance of the soldiers' uniforms and weapons is used in many other ways, from building their complicated implements to various forms of housing. It is also used as a form of currency. This substance comes from the hide of an extraordinary flat, ugly reptilian creature, rather like a scaly carpet with short stubby legs. These creatures are genetically bred to produce various sized, tough, metal-like scales, which they constantly shed and regrow. The giants exploit these animals in a shocking way, with a total disregard for the creatures that they have created. Ownership of such reptilian beasts is strictly controlled.

With a highly advanced genetic science based in power and corrupt manipulation, this giant race unwittingly creates its own doom. Spawned from their own depraved skills, the dominant giants for a long time have cloned and genespliced ever bigger versions of themselves, until finally, a killer virus is accidentally created.

I watch, as with devastating speed, the virus sweeps

through the race of giants, causing a rapid and fatal degeneration of the brain. Within thirty-six hours of contracting the virus, the giants die, totally senile. At first the victims are brutally and swiftly dispatched in an attempt to stop the epidemic, but all efforts to stop the virus fail. Within a few months, every one of the giant Beings is dead. This barbaric civilization of over three hundred million giants, which had covered one-third of the land mass of Earth, is no more.

I try again. "Treeeenieee!"

"What do you want? Why are you shouting?"

"I've been calling you over and over. What happened? Where have you been? Did you see the giants?"

A long pause. "I think I lost it for a bit. Everything went obscure for a while. I vaguely recall something about giants, but I can't make any sense of it. I think my dream state may have wandered off course."

"Boy, I'll say it did. I've been watching a race of giants killing one another. As though that wasn't enough, they tried to genetically manipulate and dominate Nature. And they succeeded—for a while. They accidentally created a virus that killed every one of them. Wow! Heavy stuff!"

"Well, I'm glad I missed it."

"Yes, maybe you were not meant to see it. It's certainly not something you need."

I reflect back on the giants, and yet again, the paradox persists. As though an itch I cannot quite reach, an inner knowing suggests that in some other frame of reality the race of giants continues, held in the Isness of Now. How this can be so, I have no idea.

I feel stunned by their culture. Part of me rages at the senseless, barbaric cruelty of the giants, rejoicing in their rapid demise, yet part of me weeps for the potential that these huge Beings might have developed.

I continue watching as the Nature of this time goes through adaptation and change. With the demise of the giants, the carnivorous reptile/horse beasts quickly become dominant, yet as the images leap forward in jumps of a century at a time, I see that these also soon die out, victims of their own implacable nature. For long ages, the Nature of Earth develops and thrives, creating many strange and gigantic warm-blooded reptilian forms—until once again, change sweeps the planet.

The Earth change that takes place this time is strange. Darkness grips the planet, while the land seems to turn itself inside out. The upheavals are somehow orderly, as though something is being obliterated deliberately. I sense that the spirit of the land needs to bury all evidence of the abominations that have lived and, for a while, thrived on the Earth. I sense a feeling of shame, but all this may well be a projection of my own emotions.

During the aeons of darkness, the planet must have tilted, for when I see it again it is somehow familiar, as though it is the Earth I know.

I try to twist around to find Treenie, but statue still, I am unable to move. "Did you see the demise of the genetically bred reptilian creatures?" I ask.

"No. All I saw was tremendous Earth changes. I'm quite certain that I was not meant to see the era of giants and what they produced or created."

The Sphere of Images

As I stare at the sphere of images, the silent, inner commentary of direct knowing informs me that I will now see our present human race. Filled to the brim, I am to be given space to digest what I have witnessed.

"Treenie, do you realize that with the exception of the giants, the one factor that has been expressed continually through all of the early human races is their love and reverence for Nature? Nature was truly their spirit Mother. I've noticed that, apart from the giants, each human race honored its relationship with Nature. This honor was based on an equality of spirit, not a motive to exploit."

"I agree. I have never seen people pay homage to Nature in such a way before. This reverence is lacking in present-day humanity. Who knows, perhaps one day you will be able to teach others how to really connect with Nature, and learn to revere it."

I inner-chuckle. "Huh! That's unlikely."

"Would you be open to such a possibility?"

"Maybe, but who would ever want to listen to me?"

"Don't be negative," Treenie admonishes me. "Why do you think all this is happening? You don't really think that this is meaningless, do you, or that there is no purpose behind it? You are here for a reason, so you had better be open to it!"

"Oh no!" I mock, "not a lecture now. Seriously, though, I really don't know how or why I am here, or any reason why I am involved in all this."

"Well, I'm pretty sure that you are going to have to make a commitment somewhere along the line, so I suggest you learn why. Experiences like this don't happen every day."

On this point, we are in total agreement! As our silent dialogue comes to an end, action begins. Once again the sphere is filled with moving images, and I see our present era of humanity. Although I am still frozen in a time lock, inside me, I weep. I watch our early primitive beginnings as men snarl and fight over women, weapons, and food. I watch men hunt animals with ever increasing efficiency, and never is there any feeling of remorse as the wild animals are ruthlessly and violently killed.

Scene after scene unfolds, and I feel ashamed. It appears that humanity, although diminished in size, has retained the brutality and disregard for Nature expressed by the earlier race of giants.

"Treenie, are you seeing this?"

A very subdued mental voice replies, "Yes."

"What do you think?"

"I'm trying not to."

Then, as humanity spreads over most of the planet, some develop into the worst types of predators, not only killing animals for food, but one another for gain and power. Finding it stark and unavoidable, I am compelled to watch.

What I see sickens me, but over and over I am getting very powerful impressions that I am looking through the narrow window of my conditioning.

"Are you seeing what I am seeing?"

"I don't think there is any doubt about that."

"I can't help but realize that I'm seeing our history through my conditioning and my belief systems. I'm looking through the tinted glass of right and wrong, of good and bad, and what

I see is a reflection of all my unrealized bias. Would you agree with me?"

"I think you put it very well. I suggest we both try to view what we see with more openness. We need to be detached, unbiased, and without prejudice."

"Prejudice. That means prejudgment of course. How many of us are capable of not prejudging? We judge before we even realize we are judging. I've been doing it all the time as I watch."

I feel Treenie's smile. "Well, you know the saying: Forewarned is forearmed!"

Gradually, by being more open, I learn not to judge what I am seeing, but to allow the images to impart a greater insight into life. I witness the impact and effect of individuality. I watch as our human consciousness becomes saturated in the concept and belief of separation. The previous earlier human races had experienced only a Oneness with Nature and all people.

I perceive now that while the giants had acted with a single accord—brutality—they also had displayed no real individuality. With a vast surge of pity, I realize that they, more than any race, had experienced and epitomized the full thrust of separation. They had felt no connection with Nature—not even with one another. The giants had undoubtedly held the potential to experience individuality, but that opportunity had been swept aside by their own implacable and unyielding nature.

I weep silently as I realize that they failed to overcome the isolation and fearfulness that separation brings with it. They were a race of victims—victims of their own inability to express love. It is love that connects us with one another, and with All Life.

"Are you crying?" Treenie asks me.

"Yes, I can't help it. I feel so sad for the giants. I realize now that they were not bad at all, but totally lost. All their incredible potential, their brilliance, and even their humanity—all lost."

"Without judgment, you are obviously seeing them very differently," Treenie observes.

"Yes," I sniff. "I guess so."

As I watch our present human race, I realize that although the potential for individuality was born in the era of the giants, it is our present humanity that is expressing it. I know now that, with the birth of individuality, the concept of separation crawled from the same bloody womb. By losing their connection with Nature, the giants were isolated and overwhelmed, destroyed by the illusions of separation.

With the birth of separation comes fear. And with fear comes desire, greed, and the resulting suffering. Because of our own subservience to separation, most of humanity no longer knows anything of Oneness, or of our connection with Nature. Humanity no longer lives with a keen daily awareness of our spiritual continuity; we live with the fear of the ultimate lie of separation—death.

I watch humanity split into many streams of expression. As spiritual individuality struggles for recognition, it is overwhelmed by ego/identity. And the power-seeking ego skillfully uses the tools of separation—boundaries and division. By using separation to create different national identities, and by inventing religion to murder, subdue, and further divide, the Oneness of humanity is splintered, fractured, and alienated almost beyond recognition.

I see again the domination of the many by the few, and I see that with civilization and religion comes manipulation and the worship of power. I watch wars and famine, rape, persecution, and imprisonment. Where the people stay communal, more primitive, their bond with one another is much closer. Only with the development of tribalism do they follow the same path of separation and domination.

Among the civilized, I watch belief systems rise, determine the way of life for a few centuries, then collapse, to be replaced by new beliefs and dogma. Among the primitive people, spiritual stories and myths of the Beginning are deeply impregnated into their consciousness, growing stronger with each passing generation.

I see the dichotomy of a civilized people expressing barbaric and savage ideals, both in religion and society, while reaping a harvest of aggression from the land—yet the primitive people live a comparatively peaceful life, with simple, spirit-based beliefs, communally sharing food that is harvested from Nature without malice. Only among the primitive people do I see a continuation of the reverence for Nature.

"It's ironic , isn't it?" I comment. "In the truest sense of the words, the primitive people are really civilized, while our so-called civilized societies are truly primitive."

"Have you noticed that humanity has now taken into its collective races all the previously separate colors of the skin?" Treenie says. "We are also simultaneously expressing an aggression toward Nature, and, paradoxically, a love for Nature."

I inner-nod. "We humans are so complex. In my deepest self, I cringe at the rage and violence of humanity. And yet, I also see love, caring, incredible self-sacrifice, and the indomitable human will."

As I see this, in all the pain, separation, and despair of a people isolated from Nature, I also see a new dynamic of growth, transformation, and change. I see past the deceit of a purely physical reality to the inner realms of Spirit. In the trauma and horror of separation and fear gone mad in an uncomprehending humanity, I see the movement of Love and Truth as dynamic forces in the growth of Soul.

I recognize a profound truth: Our deep despairs are also our unrealized triumphs, for it is then that the fabric of our potential wings strengthen beneath the cocoon of our self-deception. From our despair, Truth emerges.

With this realization ringing as a bell of exultation within me, everything changes.

The opaque sphere of images is suddenly blank, swiftly becoming clear and shimmering with light.

Simultaneously, with cataclysmic power, the water in the pressurized area is sucked upward, and before my dumbfounded eyes, the river is flowing uphill!

And I can move. In this metaphysical reality, all life is once again in movement.

3

Inexplicable Mystery

We are easily hoodwinked by our physical senses,
allowing them to fabricate and dominate our reality.
In this way, we are overwhelmed
by the apparent separation in life,
unwittingly denying our metaphysical Oneness.

Limp as an abandoned puppet, I collapse onto the river-bank. As the calm thrall in which I have been held is released, my mind and emotions are in confusion and turmoil. For long moments, I hang suspended between the heights of a transcendent joy and the depths of utter despair.

"Are you all right, my darling?"

If there is one person I need right now, it's Treenie. She comes to sit next to me on the riverbank, an expression of concern on her face.

Staring at her, I ask, "Why aren't you upset?"

She smiles. "I think you and I have had very different experiences. I have seen much the same as you, with some exceptions, but I felt rather removed from it. As I have said before, this is a dream for me."

"To me, the sphere and its images were more alive, more real than anything I have ever experienced. I feel wrung out."

"Can I help you, my love?"

I sigh. "Just being here, helps. All my years of rational, commonsense logic are unable to help me with this inexplicable and breathtaking mystical Reality. How can I even begin to analyze what is happening?"

"Maybe you shouldn't get into a lot of analysis."

"You're probably right, but I need to talk it out."

"I understand. Do you feel frightened?"

I nod reluctantly. "To be honest, yes, a bit."

"I imagine you feel rather unprotected."

"Not really, but I guess I feel vulnerable, even though my intuition tells me that my experience is being guided or overseen by a Being of Light."

"Do you fear for your safety?"

"A bit, yet paradoxically my intuition tells me that I am safer in this mystical realm than is possible in any physical reality."

Treenie smiles her agreement. "Were you upset or shocked by the images of the sphere?"

"Yes, I was, most especially by the giants and their horrendous culture. Yet my intuition tells me that I experienced no more than a fleeting glimpse of an infinitely greater mystical Reality. It has given me a whole new insight into the All That Is."

"Yes." Treenie smiles. "I see what you mean. It's only natural that you would be confused and upset though; your belief systems are all in shock. Be honest: How much of your turmoil is related to the fixed and limited belief systems that we all share?"

"What can I say? Most of it, probably all of it. Yet again, my intuition suggests that if I can accept what I am experiencing this adventure will continue, while rigidity and denial will quickly bring it to an end."

"This brings up a very important issue. Do you want it to end?"

On this I am clear. "No. Very definitely, no."

"It seems obvious that your intuition is working with a real clarity, even if you are confused. I suggest that you trust your intuition and continue with the adventure."

I give the suggestion some thought. Do I trust my intuition? After all, if my logical mind in everyday reality teaches me mainly under the stimulus of pain and suffering, surely my intuition can do better for me than that!

"I agree with you. I concede that I'm safe. I only hope that some cosmic overseer *is* in charge of all this. But by now I'm pretty sure that I can trust my own intuition."

"Don't forget, our intuition is the inner-tuition of our Greater Self," Treenie reminds me.

"It's strange," I reply. "I can feel myself accepting all this at a speed that I could never normally manage. I'm amazed at how calm I feel already."

"Be fair. You would never have such experiences to deal with in a physical reality."

"Obviously, but even so, I am now calmly accepting things that should continue to upset me for weeks."

Treenie laughs. "Be grateful, and give yourself credit. Accepting your own strength and capacity is part of our normal reality, and I bet it is essential in this."

I smile at her as I roll over on the grass. For a brief moment, my light body weakens, and I am aware of the physical me, sitting in my bed documenting this unfolding metaphysical reality. My ankle is aching from the drag of the bedclothes, and I am aware of Treenie turning over in bed next to me. Then this experience fades, and all my awareness is again focused in my light-body self, sitting next to Treenie on the bank by the river.

"I was just aware of me physically in bed, awake, and writing, and you turned over in your sleep."

"I told you that I'm in a dream state."

Treenie stares at the river as though mesmerized. "This is definitely the most extraordinary part of my dream."

Hesitant, I gaze at the river. In the precise place where the sphere had been the river is flowing smoothly upward—a vertical column of water rising from the riverbed. Impossible, utterly impossible. It's an insult to all the physical laws of the universe. But this is metaphysical! I look away hurriedly, acutely disconcerted.

"Why are you deliberately staring away from it?"

"It's impossible. Unbelievable."

"Oh, and the images in the sphere were not?"

I shake my head in confusion. "It's difficult to explain it, but this uphill river is much more challenging. I see this river every day, and it's always perfectly normal. Now, it isn't. It has gone mad! I'm well acquainted with waterfalls, but this—it's the reverse!"

"Yes, well, just take your time and relax."

"Relax, huh! Easier said than done!"

For a while I just sit in the warm sun, continually glancing at the river, then away. The sight is so completely outrageous that I need to take it in slowly.

We sit silently side by side for what feels like a long interval, when an involuntary sigh escapes my lips.

"More than anything, I am being confronted by my belief system. My belief has always been that rivers do not—under any circumstances—run uphill. This one is! I am confronted more by the lie of my belief than by a harmless river. I never once thought to include metaphysical, multidimensional realities in my belief system."

Treenie laughs. "You should have!"

"You're right. I am beginning to realize that life is as much metaphysical as it is physical. Maybe more so! Whereas my physical reality has strict limitations, it would appear that this mystical realm is without limits. We are easily hoodwinked by our physical senses, allowing them to fabricate and dominate our reality. In this way, we are overwhelmed by the apparent separation in life, unwittingly denying our metaphysical Oneness."

"How are you feeling now?"

"Much better, thanks. Your being here and helping me assimilate all this has been very necessary."

"I'm happy I can help, and I'm glad that you are all right. I don't think I am going to be here much longer."

"Don't go, please."

"I would stay if I could, but I really don't think it's up to me. You may have to continue without me. Do you reckon that you can manage?"

Even as she asks me, I feel my light body both gather strength and relax, simultaneously. Somewhere within my psyche, I have reached the unassailable Self who *knows*, and my decision is made. I can handle it.

"Yes, I do. If it's possible, I'm going to continue in this metaphysical realm. I'll accept this reality, come what may. But I would still rather have you with me."

"I'm glad."

With this decision, I feel a powerful reassurance confirming my inner strengths and capacities. And with this reassurance comes a resurgence of my intuitive knowing. Yes, I feel confident, ready for whatever awaits.

Getting to my feet, I walk over to the place where the water is flowing upward. I beckon to Treenie, and as she joins me, I notice that she is no longer so clearly defined.

"Are you still with me?"

"I can see the river, yes, but you are no longer very clear. It's as though you are leaving my dream."

I feel a bit glum at this, but the river holds my attention. Seeing it and accepting it remain challenging.

For a while we just stand there, fascinated by the stark impossibility of watching a river flowing smoothly uphill. And it is beautiful. As the water lifts from the normal riverbed, it takes on an extra sparkle and gleam, as though a bright light is shining from some hidden place behind the curtain of water. Each drop is a liquid crystal of sparkling, translucent light, flowing upward to vanish about a hundred feet above my head. Where or how it can simply vanish in space, I have no idea. Try as I might, I can see nothing beyond the top of the incredible column of water—it simply vanishes. More unaccountable, illogical, inexplicable Mystery.

And all the time Treenie is slowly fading out. Very clearly I hear her last words: "Good-bye, my darling."

For a time I sit facing the river, sad and upset. But gradually my resolve returns. Treenie would want me to continue. After all, she isn't lost or hurt. Either her dream state has left this metaphysical reality, or she is waking up. I realize that she was with me for a purpose, helping me through my initial shock and giving me the strength and clarity I so badly need. If I mess up now, I will be letting her down.

Motivated again, I jump up, and, following a strong intuitive impulse, I walk a little way further upstream. Then, trusting an inner prompting so powerful that I can scarcely resist it, I dive into the river.

Instantly, everything changes. I am no longer a human Being in a body of light; I am without form, without shape. I am the surging rush of Spirit that flows as water over every waterfall on the planet. I am falling, tumbling—water as light, light as water, water as oxygen, oxygen as water, every drop, every molecule—as One. As Spirit of Water, I am the carrier of life in everything that grows on the planet Earth. It is I who triggers the growth of every seed, I who combines with the growing plant. It is I to whom all life bows in respect, for I am the catalyst in the movement of life on Earth. All life pays tribute to the Spirit of Water, and the homage is Love. Deep in the recess of my human psyche, I recognize that the great purpose of life on Earth is to combine with, and radiate forth, the creative power of Unconditional Love.

I, the Spirit of Water, am the imperceptible, rhythmic swaying of the vast inky depths of the oceans of the world. Here, on the voice of Silence, I sing into the consciousness of the whales and the dolphins. I sing to them of Oneness, of the One life that permeates all as Spirit. I sing to them of their sister stars, of brother suns, of Light that acknowledges no darkness, of the infinity of Spirit. To the intelligent Beings of the oceans of the world, I sing, for they can hear and they can listen.

They, too, can sing. With the harmonic vibration that I invoke, they blend their energies in a resonance that uplifts and honors the Oneness of All Life. And as they sing, the oceans I am amplify and magnify the Song, blending it into a sound of Silence that reaches across all the dimensions of All That Is.

I try—oh, how I try—to reach into human consciousness. But mostly, alas, they are deaf to all Beyond. I sing my Song of Love to all humanity, for despite the ears of the heart being closed, they, too, are One with All. And to this end, I sing. And I am listened to. In a drifting, mastless boat, five people are dying. They hear me sing, for as their physical world recedes, they become open to the Beyond. Too feeble to move, they hear me sing, and, reassured, their souls release their dehydrated and decaying bodies. They hear the joy, and as wonder fills them each anew with Light, they, too, sing their Song of thanksgiving and farewell.

I sing my Song of vibrating, harmonic Silence to the children of the world, and many listen. In the new awareness that sweeps humanity, there are adults, too, who listen.

I sing to the soul, never the mind. My words of Silence are meant for no interpretation, but to carry the soul to the triumph of knowing Self as One.

In the still depths of lakes, lochs, lagoons, and ponds, I sing the endless, timeless Song of Love—the Song of creation. I touch the consciousness of every fish, of every bird, of every creature of the water—for I am the Spirit of Water. I sing my Song in every creek, stream, rivulet, and river. It is I who moves with power and grace toward the waiting sea, and it is I who awaits my coming. It is I who sings in the body of every human, every creature of the Earth, every drop of rain, each wisp of mist and fog. In every universal molecule, I am the Spirit of Water.

I sing my Song of growth within the sap of every plant, and each drop of dew is my amplifier. I stir the stony heart of every grain of sand, each pebble, rock, boulder, and mountain of the Earth. I am the bringer of the movement of life, for I am the Spirit of Water.

Without warning, my all-embracing experience of the Spirit of Water becomes centered and focused within my human psyche. I am aware of myself as One with the water, moving steadily in the current toward the place where the river flows sharply upward.

Up I flow, and up. I am the sparkling, twinkling Light in each drop of water, and I am the river as a wondrous, vital, living Whole—and I am aware of my human self, at peace with my experience.

Up, up, up, I flow—to slide with easy grace into a large pool of softly glowing, liquid light.

The Spirit of Water withdraws, and I am a man, swimming in my light body across a pool of awesome beauty. I swim with effortless ease, moving over the surface of the pool as easily as a leaf blown across a pond by some playful breeze. So sure am I that some other force is propelling me, that I stop swimming, and my progress ends. Mildly surprised, I continue swimming, using a few gentle, careful strokes. To cause splashing seems wrong, as though the disturbance might convey a lack of respect for the mystical beauty of the pool. As I swim, I hear a sound that thrills me to the very core of my Being.

It is a sound so sweet, its notes so clear, that I shiver as a faint recognition stirs within. I have heard this sound as a child, and later as a teenager. This haunting call has invaded my dreams and has thrilled me in those brief moments when a tangible reality has wavered as I reached out to Mystery. I dismissed those mystical moments as daydreams, yet I am once again hearing the Pipes of Pan—and I am not dreaming. I am aware, now, of the power of the sound. I hear not only the clear fluting of the Pipes, but mixed and merged the sound of distant wind chimes. In the merging, it seems that I can hear the faintest laughter, yet try as I might, I cannot see Pan.

My slow and gentle swimming has brought me to the shore of the lagoon of liquid light. Although this liquid light is water, so also it is far more. This is the light body of water—the metaphysical essence as opposed to its physical form. I emerge not even wet, and walk up a beach of fine gold sand—not sand of a golden color, but a beach that I somehow know is gold. As I glance around, a powerful intuitive knowing suggests that nothing here will conform to a normal reality, so I release my search for something familiar. Even so, the trees and vegetation beyond the sand appear normal enough, until I notice the independent movement of limbs and leaves in the warm, quiescent, haunted air.

Emerging from the trees, a small boy walks swiftly toward me. I stand, waiting. As he reaches me, I feel a surge of recognition, which falters. Almost I thought I knew him, but the feeling fades away.

He looks up at me. He is about six years old, his hair jet-black, but his features are not clear. In the distance, he had appeared to be deathly pale, but now I realize that his whole Being is illumined. His eyes are midnight black, but beyond that I can discern little.

"You almost remembered me," he says.

"Does that mean I know you? Honestly, I have no recollection of it. What's your name?"

"Thane."

Way down deep, something faintly stirs, then is lost. It is odd, for standing before this boy, it is I who feels like a child. The pure aware intelligence that emanates from him is palpable.

"That's an unusual name," I say inanely.

"I am here to keep you company, and maybe help you if you need assistance."

"Who are you?"

"I am an aspect of Self."

"Then I should know you!"

He shrugs slightly. "Perhaps. Do you know Self?"

I shake my head sadly. "No, I don't."

"Well, you are hardly likely to know all aspects of Self before you reach this transcendent Self-Knowing, are you?"

"That makes sense," I admit.

"Do not be hard on yourself. I am here to help you, not cause you to feel less worthy. Besides, we are closer than you could ever believe possible. We are One."

The statement bothers me, for I do not understand, but I dismiss it. I have quite enough to contend with already.

"Did you bring me here?" I ask. "Are you the Being in control of all that is happening to me?"

Thane laughs, a sound light and musical. "Good heavens, no. I told you, I am a temporary companion."

"Why only temporary?"

He smiles encouragingly. "Treenie was with you for as long as you truly needed her, as I will be with you as long as you need me. I will not be part of all your experiences, but when or if you need me, I shall be with you."

"I'll probably need you all the time."

"In that case, I had better rephrase what I said. I will be with you when truly needed, not necessarily when wanted."

"Well, thanks!" I exclaim. "That's very encouraging."

He tilts his head at an angle. "How can you resist the music of the Pipes?"

The Pipes of Pan have grown much stronger and more compelling as we talk, and I realize that each leaf of the trees, each golden grain of sand, each blade of grass, each flower and petal—all Nature —is keenly aware of this haunt-ingly beautiful sound. All life dances to the evocative power held in this ethereal resonance.

I look at Thane, bewildered. "I can't resist," I whisper tremulously.

Suddenly, a high fluting note of power, pierces me through and through, and I change again.

4

Beyond a Human Will

The great purpose of life on Earth
is to combine with, and radiate forth,
the creative power of Unconditional Love.

I am a faun, and I dance to the joy and compulsion of the Pipes of Pan. No longer do I hear an external sound, for the sound is now the rhythm of my Being. Energy of a quality and abundance unknown to my human self surges through me, my pulse beating to the inner cadence of undefined joy.

I stare at my new body with no sense of surprise. It seems the most natural, most perfect body possible. Instead of feet, I have small, sharp, pointed hooves. I feel an incredible dexterity as I pirouette and whirl to the inner beat of Pan. My legs and flanks can be likened to that of a young goat, but more shaggy, with thick, golden fur. From the waist up, I am a youth, sleek of limb and fair of face, with two tiny stubs of horns poking from the ringlets of hair on each side of my brow. No more than three and a half feet tall, I am sexless, and of a wild, tempestuous, yet divine nature.

And I can dance!

Every ethereal atom of my body is filled to bursting with the energy of Dance. I have an awareness of my Being that goes far beyond any human knowledge of Self. I am aware that the cosmic rhythm pulsing through my Being is the essence of the Dance of Life. Deep in my psyche, I recognize that this is the Song I sang as the Spirit of Water, the primal Song of Love and Joy that incubates, nurtures, and nourishes All Life. This is the Song of All That Is.

I surrender, then, to the music of vibration and energy that permeates physical, metaphysical and ethereal life. Even beyond DNA is the Song of Life—the quintessential translation of pure, divine Intelligence. My human relationship with Nature is swept away as the Pipes of Pan change my reality. Only moments earlier, the trees had been normal trees, albeit with independent movement. Now, they are columns of energy, engaged in a flow both up, toward the stars, and down, into the earth. The flow is constant, its energy defined by the seasons of a physical Earth. Sometimes strong and powerful in the movement of Spring and Summer, other times slow and gentle as Autumn and Winter energies are expressed. But never static—always there is movement.

There is also a flux of color in the moving streams of energy, color that constantly changes through the known spectrum and beyond. Irresistibly, I am drawn toward the trees, dancing as though a mote of light into the wondrous streams of energy. Had I not been held by the consciousness of a faun, I would cry out at the wonder of it. Within my human psyche, I am overwhelmed, but in my faun self all is normal and joyous.

I seem to lose my body, traveling as a mote of Light within a column of tree energy into the stars. I experience no journey or time, yet I am surrounded by countless stars, and I feel my connection with them. Overwhelmingly, the spiritual connection of All Life engulfs me, and I know that my faun/tree/human self is connected throughout the universe, and Beyond. I sense that I am surrounded by the abundant life of a multidimensional Reality. There is nothing I can see, or reach out to, but I sense the divine Intelligence.

So overpowering is the experience that, crazily, I become aware of the physical me sitting in bed, writing in a hasty scrawl as tears trickle from my eyes. Even the isolated, physical me is involved, for the joy of All That Is transcends the illusions of separation.

A quietening sweeps through me, and I am faun, dancing in and among the trees that embrace both a physical and metaphysical Reality. My experience is startlingly different from being human. My vision is more limited in some ways, more expanded in others. What I see as a faun contains no peripheral vision; I see only what I look at. However, what I see is multidimensional, for within the One, I see the All. I also feel the tree connection with the faun. This gives me a faun's view of the faun/tree reality. From this perspective, I see that each leaf on a tree is also the tree in a leaf. This connection never ends, even when a leaf falls from a tree. I am aware of a connection that transcends form and separation, for as the fallen leaf withers and dies, so the essence of the tree moves into the molecules of decay and organic matter that surround its own roots. In this way, the tree is not merely the separate form growing in a separate medium of soil; it is Self growing in Self. Living and growing, or apparent dying and decaying, are both movements within Life. To the tree, death is an illusion, for life is movement, not form. As I dance into a tree, I combine with it, *knowing* the tree in a way that is not humanly possible. And yet, I am here, and, beyond the faun, I am human!

Not only is my vision different, but also my hearing. I am no longer hearing sound outside of me, for it is within me. I hear human thought and voice from the collective consciousness, but as a faun I have learned to disengage my listening from the sound of collective human thinking. Human thoughts have become a vibration of discord in the universal Song of harmony.

On a cresting wave of insight, I realize that my faun body is a fraud, drawn from human consciousness. This body I now see and feel is only a representation of my truth, which is Light. The faun I am is a Being of Light, but so, too, is my true Self. I laugh as I realize how this experience of trees, faun, and me is possible: We are Light, we are One, as is all humanity, All Life.

With this knowing, I am once again my human self in a body of light. The Pipes of Pan are mellow now, the sound not all-pervading, and I am aware of being released from an undeniable compulsion.

"Of equal beauty is the look of wonder on your face."

I look at Thane, noticing that his illumination is even brighter than before. He obviously reads my mind.

"Your experience was mine also, and I share in your

wonder. To a lesser degree, all humanity shares this joy, this experience, but they are not conscious of it. As you so ably discovered, all life is One."

My head is spinning, and I stand staring at Thane with a grin of bliss.

It takes me quite a timeless time to come out of the pure rapture of my experience.

"Insight and clarity will surface in your awareness for many months after this, but right now, what is a first and clear observation?" Thane asks me.

I share with him the first thing that comes to mind.

"As a human, I have a freedom of will that is foreign to the faun. The faun is not enslaved or without will, but it is held within a framework of awareness and joy that compels its action. The gift of free will now has a whole new meaning for me, yet it also holds a sadness. I realize that we are not able to choose freely until we are free of the many fears that bind us to our false beliefs and endless limitations. Believing in separation denies us the full scope of our free will."

"Anything else?"

"Yes. I'm shocked—and ashamed—by the discord of our human thinking. It never occurred to me that thought produces a sound beyond our hearing, or that it could be so ugly and discordant."

"Maybe after this you will be able to think thoughts that are in harmony with the All That Is."

"I only wish!" I say longingly. But in reality I am part of the dissonance."

"Maybe, just maybe, you will have the free will to choose your thoughts."

"That's a nice thought, isn't it?" I grin. "I promise myself that one day I will. One day!"

As the sound of the Pipes fade, I look around me in awe. What an incredible place.

"Thane, where am I? Is the river a way into another kingdom? How did this all happen? Does this realm have any relationship with Earth?"

"What do you think?" he asks me.

"I think that it does. How it relates I have no idea, but I am here, and I am also physically writing this down as it happens, so this place must also relate to my physical world. But this still leaves my other questions unanswered. So tell me, how did all this happen, and the river?"

Thane smiles at me with such serenity that I feel as though I am a wayward child who never stops chattering.

"Release the questions, and you will know the answers."

"Oh fine!" I retort. "Riddles! I hate riddles."

Without waiting for my reply, Thane is smoothly walking away, rapidly putting distance between us.

Feeling a sudden exuberance of spirit, I run past the fringe of trees that lines the shores of this mystic lake, past Thane, and continue running effortlessly up a steep hill. Everything I do is so easy. I only have to think of running, and I am away, moving like a gazelle up the hill.

At the top of the hill, I pause, staring around me. As far as I can see, endless hills crest and dip into the distance, all fresh and green, and a bit alarming. Am I supposed to go somewhere or do something?

"What do I do now?" I ask Thane as he reaches my side.

"What would you like to do?"

"That's just about what I expected," I growl. "If I go wandering off in these hills, I'm sure to get lost. Will you help me if that happens?"

"What is lost?" Thane asks innocently.

"Gee, companion you may be, but help you ain't!"

Not far away, I see what appears to be a small whirlwind, but instead of being invisible air swirling round and round, it is translucent, as though filled with fog or smoke.

When I first saw the whirlwind, it was heading away from me, but it has turned, pausing. As I watch, it doubles in size, and I am disturbed, for I realize that it is aware of me and watching me.

I turn to Thane. "Er, is it friendly?"

He shrugs, smiles, and disappears.

Suddenly, the whirlwind is flowing in my direction, and I run, fleet as a deer in my light body, back down the hill toward the lake. With a high-pitched whistling, the whirlwind comes chasing after me, scattering leaves and flattening the grass as it skims over the hillside. I run, faster than I ever believed was possible, only to come skidding to a stop as I reach the shores of the lake.

Now what?

I turn to face the turbulence of the whirlwind, then I dash headlong into the trees, hoping that I can elude it. The whirlwind is moving slowly now, somehow flowing through the trees without even disturbing them. Only the odd branch twitches or waves as it passes, and I am aware that the trees are cooperating with it. I realize that it will catch me, no matter what I do, so I jog from the trees back onto the shore of the lake. There, I await my fate.

The whirlwind approaches me very slowly, deliberately trying not to frighten me. Swirling gently before me, it is now clear, sparkling with tiny iridescent lights that seem to swim within the depths of the nebulous Being—for I perceive that this is an intelligent Being that confronts me.

"Are you the Being that is overseeing my adventures?" I ask hopefully.

There is no reply. "Can you understand me?" I try.

Nothing happens. I stare hard at the entity. At least fifty feet high, it is maybe even wider, yet as I watch, I see it change. A faintly glittering tendril of breeze unfolds from the Being and approaches me. Very softly, without alarming me, it circles my light body. I feel a sense of inquiry probing me, but I don't know how to respond. Maybe I do not need to, for the gentle breeze that wraps around me has the feeling that it knows what it is about. I stand quietly, no longer afraid. The element of unknown is overpowering, but despite this, I sense that all is well. As I relax, it seems that my light body brightens. Very gently, as though opening a soft toy with a zipper, the breeze somehow opens and enters my body of light. It feels weird, as though a warm chill is moving within me. I am gently probed and prodded, not physically, but psychically.

I am aware that there is skill in this gentle inner exploration, for it is sensitive to my feelings. Somehow, the breeze touches a chord within me, and the feeling it evokes in me is experienced by the breeze. This is repeated many times, ranging from feelings of great love, joy, and amazement, to ones of fear, sexuality, anger, and even disgust. I am an open book of raw feeling, and the tendril of breeze from this strange whirlwind-like entity is able to read me.

Part of me cringes in shame at what must be revealed in some of my darker feelings, yet even as this happens, I feel an acceptance and healing from the breeze as it circles and spirals through my inner Being. Never before have I been so thoroughly examined; never have I been so exposed.

How long this examination takes, I have no idea, but there is a moment when, as though becoming a vacuum, the breeze draws me into its greater Being, and I am engulfed.

I am expanding. Instead of being enclosed in the Being, I am expanding beyond all belief. My senses are becoming more acute, my sense of Being vast. *I am* the whirling energy of Air, and in this exultation my Beingness expands tenfold.

As much as is humanly possible, I now understand the Being of Air that I am, and I know that this Being is not the overseer of my mystical experiences. I thrill, as in totally new ways I am seeing anew. I see not with vision, but by being that which I make contact with. My vision has no possible explanation, no human translation, for nothing is seen beyond Self, yet all is sensed and experienced. I am the Being of Air experiencing the human experiencing the Being of Air! I am of many dimensions. I am aware of my Beingness in many physical and nonphysical realms, and in no one place is my focus more centered, my Beingness more complete. I am truly a multidimensional Being of a vast and limitless potential.

I become aware that in my new and expansive Beingness, I am not alone. I contain an essence of all that I—the Being of Air—have encountered and experienced. In some timeless way, all that was still is, continuing in this incredible Being. I am the experience of countless elves, each a spark of joy within my Being. How long ago these were first encountered is unknowable, but in essence they remain as part of the Being of Air. I realize that I, too, will leave some essence of myself in this entity, even after I have departed, for such is the nature of this Being. I marvel at this strange Being, with its all-encompassing reality.

I am caught up by the swirling procession of elves, flowing with them in the withinness of my Being. There are elflike essences from many different dimensions, some appearing as small, solid chunks of Light, others as transparent shards of illumination, while some seem to be elfin shadows, and yet others wink in and out of reality, rather like fireflies in the evening twilight. Some are of colors that I humanly know, while others are of colors that are familiar to this Being of Air but are unknowable to my human self.

Suddenly, from within my swirling, mystical Beingness, a flock of small birds bursts into flight, flying far out into the magical countryside. And, with them, I fly. Even as I fly, I am aware that I am still within the Being of Air, for this Being seems to have no defined border of where it ends, no real demarcation. It is a reality of encompassment, of connection beyond all human definition.

I fly into a wood of tall green trees, experiencing the

essence of a small bird. Basically, I am an iridescent green, but a bright red haze seems to weave its color in an ever-shifting pattern among the green plumage. I am aware of never having been physical. In my humanness, I feel a surge of surprise, for it has never occurred to me that there may be earthlike creatures who have not taken on a physical form. The bird that I am is graceful and very fragile. I feel that I am almost crystalline, so delicate is my Being, but the Song that I contain is the power of life.

Perching on a branch of a tall, supple, willowlike tree, I sing, purely to release the joy that I contain. And as I sing, the other birds in my flock all join in. I am one bird, I am all birds, and I am the Song. Once again, I recognize the Song that I have sung as the Spirit of Water, and, again, danced to as the faun.

I realize, now, that I am an essence of the Spirit of Birds, for the Song that comes from me, and all the mystic birds around me, could never be translated into the physical sound. My Song is pure vibrating harmony. The Song is a scintilla of Truth that builds, maintains, and expresses the All That Is.

Time is meaningless. I may sing for a micro-moment, or for all eternity; each is the same. The part and the Whole cannot be separated. The Song and I are One.

I am a skylark in a physical Earth reality, singing an echo of the Song as I hover a hundred feet above my mate, where she nestles in a twenty-acre field of young wheat. In the warm spring afternoon, the sun is shining onto my mate as she lays our precious clutch of eggs. I sing to her a song of fertility and nourishment, for my Song is determined by the seasons. When the eggs hatch, I sing to the fledglings of caution and stealth, as they hide among the growing stalks of wheat. There are no words to my Song, but there is very definite meaning. In early summer, when the young are able to fly, I sing to them of food gathering and learning, and they know my Song. As autumn chases away the warmth, I sing to my young of tenacity and growth, teaching them the ways of the wild. Finally, when the soil and air are cold and the sun is weak, I sing to them of courage and survival, letting them know that the great cycle of seasons continues, and that spring is on its way. And always, no matter what season it may be, I sing in praise of the All That Is.

With a heavier, more ungainly body, I flap my way against the wind to the treetops where my mate is nesting. A harsh cawing issues from my beak, for this is my translation of the Song. As a crow, my interpretation of the Song is a joy to all of my kind. I call them to action, to the rich pickings of life. I tell them of the carrion I have found, of the places they should fly to. I caw and caw for the joy of hearing my Song, and through my Song I share myself with the other crows in my flock. I am never alone, nor can I conceive of aloneness. Even when no other crows accompany me, I am not alone, for the Song is our bonding, our connection with all others of our kind.

With the wind stroking the feathers of my face, I am an eagle high in the sky. I am alone, master of all I survey. I ride the wind with effortless effort, and I listen to the Song. In every nuance of breeze and wind as it caresses my body, I hear the Song. Only rarely do I find a need to sing it to my mate, for she, too, knows the Song intimately.

I dive, screeching with a high, keening cry as I plummet to earth. The small, immature young kangaroo is unaware of me, and as I reach it, my feet and claws extend and grasp. The young joey dies quickly, its heart pierced and its ribs crushed—such is my strength. I tear at the body for nourishment for only a few minutes before I flap my wings powerfully to lift the body into the air. Taking a slow, steady spiral, I find the thermals of hot air and rise, the dead animal limp and heavy. I know that my mate is depending on me for food, and to this end I am dedicated. I scream, high-pitched and piercing, as I share my triumph with the sky.

I am again the essence of the flock of crystalline birds. I know now that the Spirit of Birds sings its message of the One through the many. Even though it may be the beautiful uplifting song of a skylark, the harsh cawing from a carrion crow, or the death scream of a wedgetail eagle, the message remains the same: All life is One. As a human, I have gained an incredible insight, for I have experienced the movement of life from within the spirit of these birds. I have learned that endings and beginnings have no real meaning, for the deaths and births in a physical Nature do not tell the whole story of life. My insight into Nature has revealed that as an eagle, I ate only the body—a physical vehicle manifested by the spirit of my prey. The spirit of the kangaroo departed its body as I and my prey connected in consciousness. Within that fleeting moment, when as eagle I killed the young kangaroo joey, our spirits merged, nourishing in a very real way the spirit of kangaroo. The price paid was the eagle's meal. Such is *all* Nature.

With this insight, I am released from the Spirit of Birds, spiraling once more in the swirling energy of this limitless Being of Air. As a tiny breeze, I travel among the trees. Wherever I dawdle, I experience the deeper essence of whatever I linger by. I am butterfly, and I feel my Earthness. I am bee, and I feel my Earthness. I am some unknown, luminous yellow insects, buzzing in a small compact swarm near a hole in the trunk of a tree, and I feel my planet of origin as nonphysical. For an endless nontime, I touch countless insects, flowers, and plants. I absorb their essence, imparting this and how I—a human Being—experience it to the Being of Air. And within all this, I am aware of the Being of Air growing and expanding, for this—experience—is the substance of its own nourishment and growth.

I, too, am nourished. I understand, now, that in no way was I engulfed against my will by this Being of Air. The inquiring tendril of breeze read my psyche, finding the full depth and intensity of my longing to connect with the deepest essence of Nature. My commitment was such that I would willingly have surrendered my body into so-called death to experience what I am now experiencing.

Just as the Being of Air has been experiencing through my feelings and essence, so, too, it has passed its own reality through my Beingness, my psyche. Alas, like a close-mesh filter, so much has been sifted out. My experience of life is far too limited to receive more than a trace of the possibilities and potentials that this limitless Being offers me.

I weep with tears of pain for all that cannot be, and tears of great joy for All That Is.

Thane is waiting for me as I emerge from my experience. Sitting down, I allow the tears to fall, for I am over-filled and overwhelmed with mystical experience, and I need to weep it out.

More tears flow from my physical eyes as I write in a hurried scrawl. I will learn, years later, that what I am writing is a primer—the bare essence of my experience. Each word is primed to reawaken all that has happened, but only in the perfect timing of a wiser, more mature soul.

I feel compassion and concern from Thane as he sits quietly next to me, and I am grateful for his presence. I now know why he left me so abruptly.

"How do you feel?"

"Shaky. Part of me is accepting my experience with no trouble, but my emotional self is almost overwhelmed. How is it possible for my emotions to be both in the physical me, writing, and in the light-body me in this other realm?"

"Would you be whole if it were otherwise?"

"Obviously not. If I was metaphysically here, and my emotions were locked out along with my physical body, my present experiences would not be true to who I am. I would be less than whole, a false representation of the real me—whoever that is!"

"It is natural enough to feel overwhelmed."

"Overwhelmed doesn't get close to what I feel. Not only

am I overwhelmed by my experience with the Being of Air, but it's this whole weird place. Am I lost in some mystic realm, doomed to wander in other dimensions until . . . ? Until what? Can you answer that?"

"You are neither lost nor doomed, and you know it!"

I ignore him, following another sudden and disconcerting line of thought. "What happens after all this? What then? Do I carry on with my daily life as before? Do I pretend that this crazy experience never happened? Will I pretend that it was all a bizarre and wonderful dream?"

I feel uncomfortably certain that the normal everyday me will fearfully reject this, fearing the ridicule of other people. What a paradox. I suspect that my lack of self-acceptance is going to meet with unparalleled new challenges.

"What a thought," I mutter glumly. "The everyday me will be unable to accept this metaphysical Reality, or what is happening now. After all that I have experienced, I am my own greatest challenge."

"Now that's a truth." Thane nods encouragingly. "Each person is his or her own greatest challenge. Your challenge has always been to accept yourself, and what is happening to you, without your desperate need for other people's approval. In your everyday life, you will be aware of an inexplicable, metaphysical Reality that you have lived. Your challenge will be simply to accept it, even acknowledging its value."

"Don't I know it! I have a suspicion that this mystical adventure is going to bring to the boil many unresolved issues regarding my self-esteem."

"Michael, this is the beginning of a new phase in your

life. Stretching and growing will really begin when this metaphysical experience comes to an end."

For some reason, I feel an upsurge of confidence. I have learned already that all I really need is my intuition. Plus, of course, plenty of trust and a big serving of common sense. But right now, it is the matters at hand that clamor for my attention.

"You know, that Being of Air is truly awesome," I muse. "Who would have thought such an entity was remotely possible!"

"Your experience is a rare privilege."

"I'm sure it must be. You know, I thought you were odd when we first met. A child as a companion in this strange realm seemed ridiculous, although I quickly realized that you are no child. But even though you are illumined, I could relate to you. What a contrast to the Being of Air! I had never even conceived that such life forms could exist. It is beyond description, beyond definition. Somehow, in the deepest, most profound way possible, it shared its reality with me."

My term, the Being of Air, is the only interpretation I can give to such an incredible entity, but I am only hanging a label on a metaphysical Being that is so much more. For me, the entity was a whirlwind of dynamic, active air and a powerful, nonhuman intelligence—hence, my inadequate title.

"Sharing reality is a powerful communication system."

"You're not kidding! At no time did it ever communicate with me on a mental level. It shared my Beingness with its Beingness, and its Beingness with my Beingness! But it never once used words or gave me a clue about what was happening to me."

Thane nods. "You realize that you are not the same as before, nor could you be. You have been stretched, expanded, and enhanced."

"I think I must have. I learned that life in Nature, as represented on a physical Earth, is an expression of the movement of Spirit. We humans see only the physical beginnings and endings; rarely are we aware enough to see that beyond this is the spiritual continuity of All Life." I look around me, curious about such a wondrous realm, awed by its vast, all-encompassing reality.

"So what happens now? Or is it a waste of time asking? I suppose you will say it's up to me!"

Thane laughs, then shrugs. "It's up to you!" he echoes. "There is nothing you should do, or must do. There is only a metaphysical, multidimensional Reality filled with limitless potential."

"Thank you, Thane. That actually helps. So be it. In the timeless way of this mysterious place, I have only one real option, and that is to live the Mystery."

5
City of Living Glass

*Far beyond the physical DNA
there is the mystical Song of Life,
the quintessential translation
of pure, divine Intelligence.*

Together, Thane and I wander slowly along the shoreline around the lagoon of liquid light. We walk for quite a long time, if that is possible in a timeless realm.

"Are you sure you can't tell me where to go?" I ask.

"Truly, there is not anywhere you should go," he explains. "You are free to choose; life will respond."

"I believe you," I reply. "Life is that way inclined."

As my inner speculation comes to an end, I seem to walk into a cobweb of sparkling light. At first it appears as though I am enmeshed, but as I duck, trying to elude the tiny sparkles, I discover that I have inadvertently passed through some kind of membrane.

Thane is untouched, yet he is at my side. Incongruous as this is, I am covered in sparkling light, glittering as though powdered with tinsel dust. Energized, I am feeling clearer and more capable. Insight suggests that I have passed some sort of test; otherwise, the membrane would have held me back. "I suppose this would have happened no matter where I walked."

"Of course. You are the determining factor."

More than ever, I think that there is some cosmic Being in charge of all this. It's like being thrown into the ocean and then having to learn to swim. I felt for a while that I might drown, but I feel that I am swimming now. Despite this, it's reassuring to assume that someone, or something, is keeping an eye on me. I chuckle. Whoever, or whatever, chose me for this escapade must surely have a great sense of humor!

I am standing on a stretch of shore that is without trees. The sun shines unabated onto a landscape that is somehow softer, more gentle than its earthly counterpart. The sun itself is a mystery, for it is not the sun I am used to. This sun is the color of pink champagne, yet with depth and incredible clarity. Its warmth feels the same, but this sun feels as though it is very aware of me, rather than the indifferent sun of dear old Mother Earth. The air is still, but far more vibrant than our normal atmosphere. This mysterious realm is a far more energized place than our three-dimensional reality.

Before us, a steep hill rises high and wide.

"I'm going to climb to the top of that hill," I tell Thane, pointing to it.

"Oh, why?"

"Why not?" I say nonchalantly. "Besides, I should be able to get a good view of the lay of the land."

In no hurry, I saunter along, yet my lingering steps seem to carry me far faster than if I were running in a physical reality. Everything here is somehow intensified, with much more accomplished for far less effort. Effort—that's the clue. Nothing here seems to require any effort. Once I make a decision to do something, everything just flows. We could do with that on Earth! On second thought, maybe we have it, but we block ourselves.

The hillside is covered in a profusion of tiny creeping plants with pale violet buds. It resembles a very thick, wiry, shaggy carpet, so dense is the growth. There is no reassuring path to indicate that other people might walk up here, but with Thane at my side, I am not alone. Under normal circumstances, I would be breathless, walking so swiftly up a high, steep hill, but I am as fresh near the top as when I began.

With a tinge of apprehension, I reach the summit and stare in utter amazement. There before me is a small city. Right in the center, dominating the city, is a large castle. I am shocked because the city, the castle—everything seems to be made of glass that sparkles and gleams, as it bounces a million reflections of the sun. It appears that the city is moving, such is the power of the illusion caused by the ever-shifting reflections.

I stand spellbound. The city is standing on a small plateau a fair way below the crest of the hill—a city from the fairy tales of my childhood. From my hilltop position, I am able to gaze down onto, and into, its magical beauty and elegance.

"Did you know that this was here?"

Shaking his head and chuckling, Thane replies, "You still don't get it, do you? Nothing in this reality is fixed and static. This is a realm of pure response."

I glance sidelong at him. "You're right. I hear you, but I don't get it."

After staring for what seems a long time, I realize that I have seen no inhabitants in the city.

"Does anyone live here? I mean, fairies, elves, or something equally bizarre?"

"Maybe you need to go and find out."

"How come I get the feeling that I'll have to go alone?"

"Probably because that's the way of it."

I nod, already realizing it's inevitable.

"Farewell, companion," I say with heavy sarcasm, and, turning, I walk slowly toward the city.

It really is quite small. As I walk, however, my perspective keeps shifting and changing. One moment the city appears small, then larger, then it's one range of colors, then another, and so on. I suspect that it is the multicolored reflections and refractions that cause this bewildering aspect of shape-changing. Even the buildings appear like this, none of them staying constant in size and shape. It all adds to my confusion. However, as I progress into the city, one factor stays constant and steady: There is a large Golden Orb balanced on the topmost spire of the castle. How did I not see it from the hilltop, I cannot imagine. It must surely be the most dominant feature of the entire city. But everything here is odd. Only now do I notice that a hundred or more spires seem to pierce the sky, each spire the crown of a building. I don't remember seeing any of the spires from the hilltop either.

As though just emerging into my consciousness, I hear the sound of ethereal music—thin slivers of pure vibration that rise and fall with such purity that I hold my breath, so magical and compelling I dare not disturb it. And now, only now, I realize that this whole city is alive. It lives and breathes, and this music is surely its breath. How I know this, I have no idea, but there is no doubt in me: This city is a living Being. The beauty that surrounds me is so great, so palpable while remaining intangible, I just want to sit and cry, I am so overwhelmed. Human emotions were never designed to deal with such unimaginable wonder. I know now why I could see none of this transcendent beauty from the hilltop; I would have been completely inhibited.

I weep. I am unable to stop the sobs that are ripped from deep inside. There must be some mistake. Surely someone more worthy than I should be witnessing this absolute magnificence. As I weep, a soft, well-known breeze moves gently into me, touching me with its calm, familiar love, its inner healing. Gratefully, I look to see if the Being of Air is nearby, but the tendril of breeze is already moving away, its mission complete. I am left comforted and uplifted, but most wonderful of all, I feel worthy. I realize that my experience within the Being of Air has left an essence of me in its Beingness, and it has lovingly responded to my need.

Clear-eyed, no longer enmeshed in a fog of emotion, I walk slowly around this city of living glass. Somehow, now that I am hearing the music of a living city as it breathes, I am seeing anew. Or perhaps it is because I now feel worthy of my experience, but for whatever reason, the city is now revealing itself to me. I can now see that the buildings are multidimensional and that they are changing shape in a slow, constant movement that could be described as a dance. Within this movement an ever-changing blaze of color reflects endlessly from the multifaceted glass, a rippling embodiment of the Being that is the city.

For a while, I sit down to simply drink in this awesome beauty of sight and sound. There are no footpaths or paving for pedestrians in this city, no streets for traffic. Instead, it seems that it is carpeted, yet this carpet, too, is alive, rather like blue grass. It also is the Being. I marvel at the wonder of it. Here I sit on a lavender blue carpet in the middle of a moving, shape-shifting city, and it is all a single, living, breathing Being. This makes even a river that flows uphill seem mundane.

My attention is drawn to the castle, growing as it is from the center of the city. I cannot think of it as built, for its smooth lines of sparkling glass give no indication that it could be built. It is beautiful beyond any building I have ever seen, but it puzzles me. Is it a building that may be entered, or is it the heart of a Being? Only the castle remains constant, rather than shape-shift as the other buildings do. Getting to my feet, I walk over to the castle, hesitantly reaching out to touch it. I wonder if the Being will stop me, but my fingers touch the smooth surface without intervention. I gasp. The feeling transmitted into my fingertips is one of aware vibrant energy and acceptance. I realize that the substance that appears as glass is not glass at all; it is the substance of a Being. Just as my physical body is the substance of who I am in a three-dimensional reality, so this fabulous city is the body of a Being in a metaphysical realm.

The castle appears rather like a number of pencils of varying lengths, very finely pointed, and all held together in a bunch, points upward. However, the tallest of these pencils are well over two hundred feet high and as slim proportionally. Cover the pencils in a vibrant, multicolored, shimmering, glasslike material, and you have some rough idea of the appearance of the castle. Then add the large Golden Orb, impossibly balanced on the very tip of the tallest spire, far above all the others.

I gaze up at the Orb, almost mesmerized. There is a power or energy coming from the Golden Orb that is unmistakable. The Golden Orb is about the same diameter as the Sphere of Images, yet appears more solid, as though it should be heavy. Defying that impression, however, the Golden Orb is poised on the topmost needle point of the tallest spire.

Suddenly, with a soft, yet cyclopean sigh, the Golden Orb slowly splits apart, resembling an open flower with huge golden petals. From its interior, a large glowing feather comes floating out, drifting down toward me on a flake of quivering sound.

I jump back in fright, shocked. Have I violated the sanctity of the Golden Orb with my presence? Am I the cause of this? Feeling guilty, I hesitate between hurrying away and staying, not knowing what to do. Then, just as I decide that trying to avoid anything is all but impossible in this realm, the featherlike object lands on the carpet before me.

"Step on, my friend," the vehicle says in a strange, musical voice.

As though activated by the voice, the sparkles on my light body are glittering and glinting, and I feel lighter than ever before. An inner freedom sweeps through me, dispersing all my remaining doubts and lingering fear.

Without hesitation, I step onto the odd featherlike vehicle, my light body sparkling with glitter dust. I feel the apprehensive thrill of a new adventure.

Swiftly, the strange vehicle rises into the air, circling the city as it spirals higher and higher. For a few brief moments, I feel a touch of panic, then I relax. It seems as though the vehicle and I are one, so secure am I. Even when it flies upside down (to teach me?), I am safe, for it is impossible to fall off. It seems that my feet and the vehicle have melded together.

The vehicle is now drifting down toward the unroofed Golden Orb, the open petals waiting as though to embrace us. Is this how a bee sees a flower? Down we go, gracefully dropping lower and lower as we approach the center of gold. Only now, as we drift into the embracing petals, do I realize how big the Golden Orb really is. Down we go, deep into its fathomless depths, and on! Where am I? We are dropping into a haze of burnished gold, down, down, endlessly down. Finally, the craft comes to rest on a golden platform, set in a room that is vast beyond comprehension. I have the inner knowing that I am in the center of the city, yet this single room is astronomically larger than the whole city. This room must be large enough to contain a human-built city for at least ten to fifteen million people, with space to spare. How I can see its size I am not sure, but I am perceiving beyond sight, knowing beyond knowledge. And the Light! This enormous room is filled with a pulsating Light of living, burnished gold.

With a sense of astonishment, I recognize the Light. From some inner source of knowing, I realize that this Light has been shining throughout all the ages of humanity—a Beacon of Love piercing the fear and hopelessness that so often enshroud the human race. Unknown, unrealized, this Light is the herald of our greatest potential—our Awakening to our own Truth. I perceive, then, that this Light is the Light of Enlightenment. As I comprehend this, I realize that the Being which is manifest as a living city *is* the Light of Enlightenment.

I am overwhelmed with awe and reverence, yet my emotions are stable, and I no longer feel unworthy to witness such splendor.

"Open your eyes." The voice fills my whole Being, igniting long dormant senses. As though a blindfold is being removed, I am seeing with a vision that transcends my eyes, the all-embracing vision of a multidimensional Reality.

I am no longer in a room. I am somewhere in space, among the stars. But this is a space of Light, not stygian dark. Paradoxically, I can see the lights of countless stars in this Light as easily as I see them in a clear night sky.

As I hover comfortably in space, I watch countless numbers of stars wheeling around me, as though alive and aware. And I *know* that they are. Each star, as with our Earth, is an aware expression of Spirit, and each is involved in its own spiritual growth. I watch as, incredibly, the stars pause in their orbital progression in space and, without another movement, form the outline of an unbelievably immense human figure. Gradually, the details of the face are filled in—eyes, mouth, nose, ears—all with an expression of joy and amusement. The body is only hazily defined, as though unimportant.

I gaze in awe at a human figure of sparkling stars that is bigger by far than the Milky Way, and I gasp. Almost as though compelled, I see that in a minute way, I, too, am a human figure of sparkling stars, for the glitter dust is now whirling and orbiting around my body of light. A connection takes place in consciousness, and, with an explosion of insight, I see the full magnificence of humanity. I *know* that we, too, are Gods of Creation. On a crest of insight, I realize that this Limitless Being *is* the Light of Conscious Enlightenment, a representation of the Beings that we, in the continuing development of our spiritual evolution, both already are and will eventually become.

While absorbing and assimilating this incredible truth, I am held in a cocoon of Love, protected from the shattering impact of what must be the ultimate paradox: We already are what we are becoming. I accept this, for in its perfect moment of timing, Truth is undeniable.

I watch as lips that encompass the heavens smile at me. I listen as omnipresent words of power reach out to me, carried on a surge of thunder, which, beyond sound, is the vibrating nexus of everything I see.

"My child, you are now born into Truth. But you must bring about your own Awakening, and know Self."

The words cease, and from those lips an arrow shaft of Light reaches out, piercing me to my soul. Deep within me, I feel a formless pain. Then it fades. Against my will, I see the everyday me exposed — my folly, my fears, my humanity. I *know* that every aspect of me is loved by the

Light of Enlightenment. There is no judgment, no condemnation—only complete acceptance. This *is* Love, absolute and unconditional.

But me, I am my folly and my fears and all that makes me human, and I cannot accept my humanness. With tragic insight, I realize that in this moment I have just missed an opportunity to *know* Self, to "fall in Love" with Self.

I watch as new worlds float out from the same vast mouth that spoke to me. I see these worlds creating new orbits and, coming together, forming new galaxies. I know that I am watching creation, and I know that I and all humanity are both a part and the whole of this creativity, and yet I am held captive by my own limitation. I have the knowledge, but I am not yet able to live and express the *knowing*.

The vast figure abruptly vanishes as the stars are once again orbiting in space, each following its own continuum. I am acutely aware that the figure was formed for my benefit, encouraging me to see past the forms of life into the very nexus of creativity.

Everything blurs, space vanishes, and I am standing alone in the immense room of blazing Light. I am quite sure that this Light is reflected in the spirit of every human Being on Earth, and that the Golden Light purposely shines, forever undiminished, for each one of us. I feel certain that this realm I have entered is where many of us come in our deepest dreams, when we seek inspiration and comfort beyond the physical plane.

I wonder what the words I heard will mean to me: "You are now born into Truth." I don't feel any different. I already knew I have to Awaken; I have been trying for years!

And the Light that pierced me, what does that mean? I notice that although my light body is still sparkling with glitter dust, it is no longer spinning and orbiting around me. I feel sad and despondent, knowing that I have missed an opportunity to Awaken, and feeling as though I have fallen from some high pinnacle of divinity.

Without warning, high-pitched laughter echoes around the vast room, and, suddenly, it seems the whole place is alive and moving. How wonderful, how absolutely marvelous! The room is ablaze with a myriad of tiny elves, each about the size of a bumble bee. They seem to deliberately catch the Golden Light, reflecting it in countless miniature rainbows as it bounces from one moving elf to another in a never-ending crescendo of light and color. Their laughter is wildly infectious, and I smile, then laugh aloud.

A small swarm of the tiny fairy Beings hover before me. Each is composed of Light, holding no defined form for more than a few moments before winking out, to wink in again micro-moments later. It seems that they simultaneously occupy two different dimensions, continually zipping in and out of each. I feel their joyous energy as a wave of refreshment, and, spontaneously, I am leaping up and down with them, dancing with the abandonment of a clown.

To my astonishment, I am no longer standing on the floor; I am flying. Surrounded by a huge swarm of the tiny elves, their laughter ringing in my ears, I am flying around the room, as lightly and effortlessly as a dragonfly. Without any waving of arms or movement of limbs, I am flying simply because I want to fly. I zip in and out of clusters of elves, and they in turn swirl in a cloud of sparkling light all around me. As I fly, I realize that this is no different from the stars whirling around the vast figure in space — except in size. For moments I hover on the edge of some vast insight, but it eludes me. Unconcerned, I laugh with the sheer exuberance and joy of effortless flight, while the elves gather around me and, in a huge cluster, we all zip out through a wall of the castle as though the wall is no more substantial than a cobweb. Swooping to the ground, the swarm of magical elves deposit me outside the castle, vanishing on a receding wave of high-pitched, impish laughter. I jump into the air to follow them, but light though I am in my light body, I cannot fly, much as I want to.

Curious, I walk over to the castle and touch a wall. It feels as it did earlier, aware and accepting, but unyielding. Stepping away, I gaze up at the Golden Orb. It is again intact, a perfect sphere of Gold. Unsure of what to do, or where to go, I decide to walk back to Thane.

Leaving the castle, I walk through the city and out, heading toward the hilltop. I plan to meet Thane and then walk back to the lagoon of liquid light, for that is where I entered this realm. It represents my only real connection with a physical reality and, perhaps, a way out.

As I walk up the hill, I notice that the violet flowers of the wiry, creeping plant are wide open. Gazing at them, I remember that earlier they were mostly in bud. The air is filled with their fragrance, a subtle aroma that I have never before encountered. It seems that the fragrance somehow invokes memories, but these memories must surely belong to someone else. Images of a huge orange sun fill my mind, a sun so close and large that it fills half the sky. Rather than external heat, I seem to remember a glow of warmth inside me, an energy of inner nourishment.

I stop, my hands holding my head as though to forcefully pull greater clarity from my mind, but it is all slipping away. The memory of a slender people with almost translucent blue skin dances tantalizingly before me; then it is gone.

Bemused, I walk on, reaching the top of the hill.

Reclining among the violet flowers, Thane seems lighter, somehow brighter than ever.

"You seem really lit up," I say.

He nods. "Yes, I must leave you very soon. Despite your apprehension, you are proving to be very adaptable and capable. You really do not need me."

I am dismayed by his words. I do not want him to go, but I am aware that what I want makes little difference here.

"Before you go, tell me one thing. Are there any 'nasties' here?"

"Michael, in all truth, the only 'nasty' is if you were to manifest your fears. What you fear you both create and attract. This is a truth in your physical reality, and it remains so in a metaphysical Reality."

I feel reassured, but other questions clamor for the relief of being answered.

"What or where is this place? How can a river flow uphill to this land of mystery? How can there be a land up here? Where is up here?" I sigh, knowing Thane will not give me any satisfaction.

"Easily answered, Michael, and in your own words. Live the Mystery. That is the only solution available to you."

"That's about what I expected. That's like following the yellow brick road! Follow it, and trust."

While Thane is speaking, he is somehow becoming brighter, and yet more faint. It is rather as though a light is shining through him, and he is dissolving into the light. "Good-bye, Michael."

"Wait. Will we meet again?"

Very faintly, he answers, "Yes, but you will not remember me." And then, very strongly, he adds, "Remember, I am an aspect of Self. We are One."

He has gone, and I feel lonely, yet, oddly enough, I do not feel alone.

Relaxed, I lie back among the flowers. Trying to work out the hows and whys of this place is way beyond me. At least there are no "nasties" waiting to snatch me up.

Dreamily, I wonder if, or when, the mystery Being who got me into this realm will show up. Meanwhile, all I can do is enjoy the wonderment. How astonishing—to be able to experience other forms of life, where "I" am not even "me."

I stare at the Golden Orb balanced on its needle spire. One thing is certain; the distance I dropped into the castle in no way equates with the height of the castle. I'm certain I entered yet another reality. Where does it all end? Does it end? Somehow, I don't think it does.

6
The Gates of Time

Like a flower unfolding its petals
from a tight bud,
constantly increasing in size and volume,
so our inner knowing can come into bloom.

S tanding on the familiar hilltop, I turn around to have a last look at the city and stare aghast. The city has vanished! Nothing exists to indicate that it was ever there. Even the landscape of hills has vanished. An undulating plain of short, pale green, fine-bladed grass stretches out before me, with not the slightest evidence that it was ever different from this. Despite the bizarre and outrageous encounters I have had, I am again shocked!

Turning around, I look toward the lagoon of liquid Light. It would not surprise me if this also has vanished. But no. I can see the water sparkling far below me at the bottom of the hill. Feeling relieved, I wonder if that is where I should go. This place is so bewildering, and with no guide I am really perplexed.

Turning back, I gaze once more at the vacated city site. Wonder on wonder! A pair of vast silver Gates has appeared, hundreds of feet wide and as many high. Impossibly huge, the Gates are slowly opening, while a faintly glowing purple light pours through them.

Even where I stand, I feel a quickening of the energy

around me. It feels as though the air has become mildly electrified as tiny tingles course over my light body. The purple light hugs the ground, like a fog rising from the soil, but no earthly fog was ever purple, nor did it ever glow with vibrant energy. With a further shock, I see a number of people coming through the Gates, laughing and talking with one another.

As I stare, they wave to me, beckoning me to join them. Slightly hesitant, I walk toward them. The idea of more company is suddenly not quite so appealing, for as I approach them, I feel increasingly inferior and insignificant.

They wait, smiling at me as I walk deeper into the field of glowing purple light. I gaze at them in awe. While not giants, these are big people, all well over six feet tall, and with perfect bodies. And I mean perfect! They are so perfect they are like the living sculptures of a Michelangelo. But equally stunning is the radiance of pure vibrant energy that each one possesses. The women are beautiful beyond any female beauty I have ever encountered, while the men are virile and handsome. Their clothing is all very similar; both male and female alike are wearing white, short-skirted tunics. They remind me of a subject I used to be deeply fascinated by as a boy—the Gods of Greek and Roman mythology.

Stunned, I falter to a stop. These *are* the Gods I used to read about. These are the mythological Gods of my youth. Vivid images spring to mind of the hours I used to spend reading about my Olympian heroes. They were my escape from the world when I was in trouble or bored, but they also became friends and comrades who inspired and excited me. I did not realize it at the time, but they served to stimulate my imagination and visualization as their images came to life. I used to see these Gods in my mind's eye as clearly as I can see them now. Just as I used to imagine them, they all have perfectly tanned golden skin, as though fresh from the solariums of Hollywood, and while the Gods all seem to be dark-haired, the Goddesses are all blond. Without doubt, they look like Gods, and they have the aura of Gods, but I am perturbed because I now realize that they are the most stereotyped Gods I have ever seen.

"You have seen other Gods, have you?"

The man who is asking the question regards me with twinkling green eyes.

My jaw drops slack, as I stare mutely at him.

With one hand held high, his finger pointing before him like a stylus, he writes the sentence in the air: "YOU HAVE SEEN OTHER GODS, HAVE YOU?" Each yard-tall letter and word is made of dense white light.

I gulp. "Er, no," I gasp.

He chuckles. His body, which appears so youthfully God-like and masculine, blurs slightly, reappearing as much older, bigger, and bulkier, and with an aura of greater wisdom. He is now white-haired and bearded but still virile and powerful.

"Do you recognize me now?" he asks.

This is all too much for me. I am overwhelmed. The God standing before me, a wide smile on his face, is the exact image of Zeus that I used to visualize as a boy.

"Zeus," I say weakly.

Laughing aloud—a thunderous sound as though fifty people are laughing—he blurs slightly, to become again a youthful, golden-skinned God so similar to the others. All my lack of self-esteem comes boiling to the surface, and I feel as worthless and reduced as pulped cabbage. I am so threatened by their overpowering presence and beauty that I cringe inwardly.

A Goddess looks reprimandingly at Zeus. "Enough of your jesting. Can you not sense his feelings?"

She comes to my side, takes my right hand, and, raising my fingers to her lips, kisses them. A bolt of clean, pure energy passes through me, as though an electric shock. My own light-body aura, which has been severely reduced by my feelings of inadequacy, again glows brightly.

"There is a lesson in this for you, Michael," the Goddess says, her eyes on mine.

I know instantly what she means. When I think of myself in a deprecating way, I reduce myself, and my light diminishes accordingly. Although I can see the effect when in my light body, exactly the same is happening when I am the physical me. Why do we humans spend so much time reducing our light instead of increasing it?

"Who are you?" I ask her.

She smiles. "We have neither names nor identities, although we have had many of both. None of them was ever real. Rather than identifying us as the Greek and Roman Gods that are in your mind, think of us as the symbols of your potential."

"Please, who were you?" I persist.

Laughing aloud, she confirms what is in my mind. "I was

Persephone, whom you so admired. But, as you must by now realize, I am in this image only because you hold it in your mind. Like he whom you perceive as Zeus, I can change in character and gender. I repeat, we are symbols of your human potential dressed in the garments of human myth. However, for your benefit, we will let you gaze briefly on the heroes and heroines of your youth."

Suddenly, they are all around me, and I am acutely aware that they are laughing *with* me, not at me. Here, just for me, are the larger-than-life images I idealized and admired so much as a boy. The massive figure of Zeus, father of Persephone and Perseus and of many other Gods; Mars, the great Roman God of war, and Thor, the mighty Norse God of war; Perseus, the slayer of Medusa, a Gorgon; the beautiful Helen of Troy, who caused a war; Hermes, the winged messenger of the Gods; Jupiter and Juno, father and mother of many of the Roman Gods; the great Pan, the God of Nature whom I most loved; Persephone, a Goddess of such beauty that she was taken by Pluto, God of the Underworld, to live with him, but each year she returns as Spring; Narcissus, who fell in love with his own image and, for a while, frightened me of looking into a mirror; and Hercules, my greatest boyhood hero, who labored so mightily and thrilled me so deeply with his massive strength and fantastic deeds.

These and others whom I read about are gathered around me, fulfilling a boyhood wish that I never even knew I had. Taken from my mixed and muddled memory, this mishmash of Greek, Norse, and Roman Gods represents all that I most admired and ever aspired to as a boy.

Two realizations are tearing at me. First, that I no longer honor the mythological memories in the way that I did as a boy, for most of them are no longer valid in my adult reality. Second, I am shocked that the Gods have formed a big circle around me, and they are bowing to me! Without warning, the circle of Gods is shimmering and blurring, then it stabilizes. No longer manifesting their energy as the immortals of mythology, they now appear as ordinary people in everyday clothes. Relief rushes through me in a cool wave. Although I recognize that these are Great Beings, I can more easily relate to them as regular people. But they are still bowing to me!

I gasp. Who am I that Beings such as these should bow to me? A man, with eyes as black as jet, set in a lean, hawkish face, approaches me. Reaching out, he very gently touches my eyes, and as though another veil has been drawn aside, I again see anew. With this greater clarity of vision comes a direct knowing. Far surpassing any normal understanding, I directly know. Like a flower unfolding its petals from a tight bud, constantly increasing in size and volume, so my knowing is expanding within itself. I know why these exalted Beings are bowing to me, for I, too, can now see the Light that shines from my heart. They bow not to me, a single human Being, but to the Light of Humanity, which I represent.

The Light that pierced me when I faced the Being of Enlightenment among the stars was not a momentary thing, to fade away. The Light is a catalyst. It reawakened my knowing that this Light is carried in the spiritual heart of every human Being, and no matter how despairing his or her situation may be, the Light never falters. It is a beacon not of hope, but of Love. It is a reminder not of physical values, but of our spiritual Self. It is the Light of our divinity that beckons us, reminding us of our birthright. It is a Light that never diminishes, no matter how ignored it may be or how long it may take to discover. No matter how much we abuse ourselves or are abused by others, the Light shines unabated, untarnished. This Light is the nourishment of Truth, our truth. The Light shines, and we *are* the Light.

Tears spring to my eyes. Only with the gift of true sight do I realize how limited our normal seeing really is. I know that *true* sight contains an accompanying *insight*, and that this is the potential of all humanity in our everyday life. We grope in the dark in more ways than one. With this gift, I see now that the Great Beings are truly Beings of Light, for the aura of Light that emanates from them is tremendous. Happily, I no longer feel reduced or threatened by their magnificence. Instead, I feel uplifted and magnified simply by being with them.

Respecting the revelations that are sweeping through me, the Great Beings are now conversing in small groups. Little is spoken aloud, but my new insight allows me to participate in the wordless exchange that is directly shared among them. So complete and whole is this directly imparted communication that there is no possibility of misunderstanding.

As I walk among them, I am surprised that they respect and value what I have to share. Realizing I am a regular human, living with the struggle of everyday life on a physical level, they are interested in my observations. On a one-to-one basis, and in groups, they share their clarity and knowing with me. For me, this comes across as a potential for our future, both on a personal level and for humanity. Visions of potential arise as bubbles of insight within me.

With surprise, I perceive that despite the constant violence of human to fellow human—of our often obscenely inhuman treatment toward other humans—we are honored by these Great Beings. And I discover why. These Great Beings are without judgment. It is our judgment of our families, neighbors, and friends that creates our isolation and fear. It is the judgment by each nation, culture, and religion of other nations, other cultures, and other religions that creates our fear-based wars. And it is our judgment of our own self that, by isolating us from our greater Truth, denies us a true inner peace. Without judgment, the Great Beings love and accept us. They know that judgment separates and isolates and that this is the breeding ground of fear and contempt.

Feeling the melancholy that is creeping into me, some of the Great Beings embrace me, sweeping me effortlessly off my feet as they whirl me around, and my whole perspective changes. I am filled to a joyous overflowing with the realization that, inevitably, humanity will break free of the bonds of separation, with all its false illusions and its many attendant fears, and we will know our God-Self. This is our destiny, our birthright.

It has become obvious that these Great Beings can easily monitor my thoughts and emotions. They know when inner realizations burst into my awareness, and they know the truths that expand within me. With this knowing, they offer me a gift. They tell me that if I wish it, they will place me in spheres of direct experience. This will have the effect of transforming my mental insights into actualized reality. But I have to choose this freely.

"Will it hurt? I ask.

"Does all experience have to hurt?" the one whom I knew as Zeus asks.

"Yes," I reply. "Humanity is hot-wired to pain and suffering, and I am no exception. It seems to be the only way we ever really learn anything." I smile sadly. "I guess we get so much pleasure when the pain stops, we eventually learn our lessons. That's why I ask if it will hurt."

Zeus places his hand on my shoulder, squeezing firmly.

"Yes," he says kindly, "it does seem to be the human way, but it has never had to be like that. The choice of Love has always been available. By not choosing Love, the choice of suffering is inadvertently made. Is Love so difficult a choice?"

In this moment, my insight far exceeding my ability to live it, I know why it is so difficult. "When fear dominates our lives, separating us from our own truth, then it is fear that chooses, and fear never chooses Love."

Nodding gravely, Zeus looks deep into my eyes. "I respect what you have said. The spheres of direct experience will seem real, and, indeed, they will be real, yet reality has many facets and dimensions. You will feel pain if that is contained in your experience, but it will not be the pain of your physical reality. Your physical body will remain safely in your bed, and your light body will be safe here with us. You, however, will live the experience in full reality."

"How is that possible?" I ask.

"Believe me, it will be as real as anything you have ever experienced. The how of it is irrelevant."

The prospect the Great Beings offer frightens me, but painful or not, there is no way I can pass up this opportunity and continue to live with myself.

"You have my solemn promise that you will come to no harm," Zeus tells me, already knowing my choice.

"Wait, I have a question for you," I say hastily. "Was it any of you who brought me into this realm?"

"It was not us," Zeus assures me.

So saying, I notice that he has a fist-sized crystal sphere in his hand. He holds it out so that I can see it.

"That looks just like a miniature version of the Sphere of Images," I say.

Zeus gives me a smile of acknowledgment. "It should. Tell me what you can see in it."

I stare at the sphere intently . . .

. . . and fall straight into the scene that is within the crystal sphere. I am a crofter, in a long ago England. I toil on my land from daybreak until dark, and toil and work are my whole life. Work has made me dour and grim, my once black hair is now graying, and my features have become harsh and frozen. I have a wife and five children, and life is very hard. My wife Ellen is crying as I enter the doorway into our small stone hut. Perched in the lee of a hill on the Yorkshire dales, the winds try in vain to shake our rough but strong hut.

"What's up now?" I ask.

I am tired to the bone, sick and tired, and impatient with the ways of a woman.

"Tom's dead," she says, her voice carrying her pain.

My legs give way, and I collapse onto a wood bench.

"Dead! Dead!" I say stupidly. "He can't be dead. He only got the chills."

"The chills have killed him, just like Charlotte, and Elizabeth, and Raleigh. And now George has it . . . and you are so sick you can hardly work."

The pain that I have been holding is too much, and, lurching to my feet, I rush to the door. It is late afternoon, and as I run blindly outside, the sun hits full into my eyes. Tears from my broken heart mix with the tears of dazzlement, and I sink to my knees.

"Oh Lord," I whisper, "why do you give us so much to bear?" My voice rises to an angry shout, "WHYYYYYYYY?" I listen as the echoes bounce my question from hill to hill: "YYYYYYyyyyy."

Blood flecks my mouth, and my cough begins again, a harsh, wracking cough that is tearing my lungs to pieces as I spit the phlegm from my lips.

"Lord, who will take care of the family when I am gone? How will this end?" I am coughing and gasping.

Ellen is suddenly beside me, holding me, wiping the blood from my lips. "Tom, Tom, Tom," she murmurs. "Oh, Tom, my poor, poor Tom."

I cry deep, wracking sobs of undiluted misery. I am so overburdened that I am broken. Child after child has died, and now my little Tom. He was so like me, with my name, the same eyes, and the same stubborn jaw. Only mine isn't stubborn any more. Like a stick snapped in the hands of some careless giant, life has broken me. I'm ready to die. I'm truly beaten.

I'm so old. At fifty-five, I'm old and worn-out, yet dying is so delayed, so prolonged. I have been dying for nearly three years, and still I live to suffer more. I don't understand. My children grow to be strong and in their teens, and—puff—they are sick one minute, then dead. And Ellen, my lovely Ellen. She was the beauty of the dales only a few years ago. Now she is ravished by hardship, made gaunt by the death that surrounds her, struggling to keep her sanity in a life plagued by sickness and death.

Mentally, physically, and emotionally exhausted, I slump to the ground, sinking into a fretful slumber right there on the soil outside our shack.

I dream. I dream that I am looking into a still pool of water, and I clearly see a person gazing back who looks like me, yet doesn't. I watch, dazed, as he steps out of the pool and confronts me. This person is not beaten by life and time. He is upright, not stooped, and his face is smiling, not scowling. He can't be me, yet I know he is. His smile is very friendly as he meets my eyes.

"Hi, Tom. How's it going?"

"Bloody awful," I tell him.

"Bad choices, Tom," he says.

"What bloody choices have I ever had? Fool."

"That is a choice, Tom. Why call yourself a fool? If you call yourself a fool, and believe you are a loser, and believe you are beaten, do you know what happens?"

"I have bloody bad dreams."

"Wrong, Tom. You *live* bloody bad dreams."

"Who are you?" I ask.

"I am the you that could have been. I am another aspect of you. I am both your lost past and your possible future. I am your fullness, while you are your decay. I see how good life is; you see how dreadful it is. What you see in me is in you, but you are unable to accept it. I am your positive potential; you are living your negativity. Does that help explain, Tom?"

"I must be dying," I retort.

"You would like that, wouldn't you? Death is not all that you think it is. You think that in death you can escape from all this, abdicate your responsibility. But you are wrong. You will continue, Tom, and anything that is unresolved will have to be faced again. You create your own pain, your own joy. How much joy have you had, Tom?"

"If you throw a pebble in a pond, ripples spread across the surface. Those ripples are life, Tom, and they continue through one life cycle after another. If they contain suffering, death will not end it. Just imagine, you may have to do all this suffering again. How do you feel about that, Tom? Would you like more of the same?"

"You're a liar. This is the Lord's lot that I have to live. I am a God-fearing man, and this is my lot."

"That's baby dribble, Tom. Pure sheep shit! If you fear

God, then fear is your reality. And, by God, you will have plenty to fear. This is your lot because you create it."

"How do you know all this?" I ask angrily.

"I know because, in your heart, you know."

I stare into the pool, beaten, tears streaming from my eyes. Deep inside, I know he speaks the truth. Because I have never lived that truth, I have tried to reject it. But now, I am at the end of the road.

"I don't want this as my lot. Please, please, I beg you, can you help me?"

"Do you really want help, Tom?"

Somehow, in my dream, I know that this is my last hope, my last chance. And I do want help. Although I don't really believe that I would come back to this again, just the risk of repeating this suffering is too much to bear. And this other me could be right!

"Whoever you are, please help me."

"Look at me, Tom. Really look. Look at me as though you have never seen yourself before. Look at the newness of me, the power of me, the Light I am, and most of all, see the Love of me."

I stare at my embodied reflection and, glory be, I can see afresh. This other me has a smile that lifts the spirit. He has an aura of power—not personal power, but a power that comes from within. It is a power that lights him, and as I gaze at him, I feel ignited. And I not only see love shining from him, I feel that love. Even in this dream, I feel Love like a power, and it is entering me!

I sigh. My eyes open, and Ellen is cradling my head and shoulders as I lie slumped on the cold soil.

I look up at her. "I had a dream. An incredible dream."

Ellen smiles at me, and for the first time in many a year, I really see her. She is not ravaged by hardship at all. Instead, I see now that her features are strong, powerfully sculptured by the challenge of life. She is lean, yes, we all are, but her leanness becomes her, and I can feel the strength in her fingers as she grips my shoulder. I see into her eyes, and I am shocked. I see no sign of defeat, only the pain of having to support a weak husband. And I see her love and willingness to do this.

I take a long, slow breath, careful not to start the coughing. "Ellen," I say, "I love you more than I have ever said and more than I have ever realized. Will you forgive me for being defeated even before you and I began our life together?"

She is crying now. "Don't die, Tom. Please don't die," she gasps. "I've always loved you. I've always seen what is possible for you, but you never could."

I smile, the first real smile in a long time. "I met him, Ellen, my love. I met the possible me in my dream. He told me how it's possible for this me to become the possible me. And you know what? With your love and help, I think it's possible!"

I am standing in front of Zeus, staring into the tiny crystal sphere. Dragging my gaze from the sphere, I look at him dazedly. My mouth opens and then closes. I stand for a few moments, speechless, collecting my wits.

"Ouch," I finally say. "That's emotional pain."

He smiles sympathetically. "How do you feel?"

"I feel good," I say truthfully. "Did that really happen? I get the feeling that I was once the peasant farmer and that Treenie was once Ellen."

"To be accurate, what you experienced *is* happening. Yes, you *are* the farmer and Treenie *is* Ellen," Zeus replies.

"But . . . how is that possible? This was England several centuries ago. And how can Treenie and I be two other people in a different time at the same time that we are us living now?" I ask him.

Zeus laughs, his long dark hair bouncing in the waves of pink sunlight. "You do have a way with words!" He chuckles.

He holds the sphere before me. "Imagine that this sphere is filled with dust. To give me the license of explanation, you could say that all the dust occupies the same space. Every one of these countless specks of dust represents a cycle in the Wholeness of your life. You call these cycles lifetimes. They all occupy the same no-time framework together. Who you are—Self—experiences all the life cycles of your individual identities simultaneously. However, for this to have real meaning for the identities who you believe yourself to be, each life cycle is experienced in a linear procession, thus creating the illusion of time. To be fair, time *is* valid for a physical, three-dimensional reality. The illusions only begin when you believe that this limited reality is all that life is and also when you forget that all humans are really metaphysical, multidimensional Beings of Light."

"Phew!" I exclaim. "But I think I get it. Tom is an aspect of Self in exactly the same way that I am. He thinks he is the only Self, just as I always have. And the same applies to Treenie, and to everyone. So if all time occupies the same space, then each life cycle is a different, yet simultaneous reality. This suggests that linear time is the device that appears to keep it all apart, thus allowing each aspect of Self to develop and grow. In this way, Self grows also. How's that?"

Zeus laughs, clapping me on the shoulder. "Excellent. Now, how would you like to return to Tom and Ellen? You may be interested in their development. After all, Tom also is an aspect of the Self you are."

"How did I get into that other reality so easily?"

Zeus holds up the small sphere in his hand. "To take license again, you could say that this crystal sphere is programmed to open the Gates of Time."

I indicate the enormous silver Gates through which all the Great Beings appeared. "You mean like those? Are they the Gates of Time?"

He grins. "Only in as much as my term, the Gates of Time, is a metaphor."

Holding forth the crystal sphere, he asks, "Ready?"

I lean forward, peering into the sphere.

Two years have passed. I have never forgotten the dream I had, following the death of young Tom. Strange things have been happening and I have learned so much. I nearly died soon after that dream. My life hung in the balance for a while, and Ellen had to sell a few of our best ewes to pay for medicines. But we were very blessed. An old Romany woman came to see us at the time I was close to death. She told us an incredible story. She said that she had been my father in a previous life cycle and that she had treated me very badly. As my father, she had broken my spirit. This was the reason that I had found my life so difficult. Now she had come to repay her debt, for her past error was a heavy burden that she had carried. She was a very skilled herbalist, and she was certain that she could help me recover, but she told me that I, too, must change my ways. I had to surrender my gloomy, pessimistic views and be more optimistic and open about life.

I told her about my dream. She was astonished. Apparently it was not my dream that surprised her but that the same person—me—who had come to me in my dream, had also come to *her* in a dream and showed her the past life that she told me about.

She was a wise old woman and a marvelous healer, and when she went out of our lives, I was a healed man. The last thing she asked of me was that I forgive her for what she had done when she was my father. I told her that not only did I forgive her but that she was welcome to live with us for the rest of her life. She declined, saying that traveling was her way, but she and I hugged, sharing our love, each freed from the bonds of the past.

Before we parted, she told me something incredible. She told me that I had healed myself. She said that her herbs had repaired the damage to my lungs, but that it was I who

107

did the healing. She told me that this is the basis of all true healing.

I believe her, because I am living proof. It was not easy to change the old pattern of my thoughts, but with Ellen's help, I did it. Is it because of me that George got better also? I have to ask the other, more terrible question. Was it because of me that our other four children—Charlotte, Elizabeth, Raleigh, and young Tom—died? Although I do not let it control me, the question haunts me for nearly a year. Then I have another dream.

I am standing by that same pool again, staring at the reflections. Instead of it being my reflection in the water, I am astonished to see my tall, lovely Charlotte, my sweet Elizabeth, my strong but always sad Raleigh, and heavens above, my beloved young Tom. Overcome, I weep.

As before, they also step out of the pool.

"Father, please don't weep," Elizabeth pleads. "The time for weeping is finished. We have come to tell you that you were not the cause of our deaths. You remember learning about the ripples in the pond, don't you? Well, we also had cast our stones in previous lives, and the way we died was from what we, too, had cast out. This is the way of life, Father. You simply provided us with the situation we had helped to create."

"It all fits in, like dovetailing two pieces of wood," Raleigh adds. "When you tend your sheep, Father, realize that every sheep has its place in the flock. No sheep is a random factor in the flock; each has its perfect place." He smiles one of his rare smiles. "The human flock is no different; we are each in the place of our choice."

"On a soul level, I knew that my death would be the last straw," says Tom. "My death would either break you completely or it would be the catalyst for your change. Father, we are so delighted that you have changed and grown, for that makes our lives and our deaths worthwhile and meaningful. Thank you, Father."

"We are here, now, because we love you, Father," Charlotte adds, "but it is you who have made all this possible. Your healing is our healing, and your change is also ours. We are never separate, never alone. Good-bye, Father dear. God bless you."

Suddenly, they are within the pool, and I watch as the reflections blur, and in the odd way of dreams, four beautiful swans appear on the pond. Each stands high in the water, startling white and pure, beating its wings back and forth as though just liberated. I watch as the swans rise from the pond, circle over me once, and then fly high and far away. I weep again from the sheer joy of what I have witnessed. Then I awake.

Do we create our own miracles? I'm convinced now that we do. With my return to health, plus a changed attitude and outlook, even the weather seems to be more favorable. Or perhaps it just seems that way since I have learned to count my blessings. Our small farm is now thriving, and my fine flock of sheep is the envy of the other crofters. Ellen and I are closer than we have ever been; it truly is a life renewed. What a fine, strong woman I married! With her help, I am now a man of love instead of fear, and we both reap the harvest of love.

I learned one other lesson. Whereas before I seldom

mixed with people or got involved with other crofters, and had few friends as a result, I now give much of my time to friends and neighbors. I have learned that as they prosper from my advice and help, so, too, do I. I have learned that what we give to others, we give to ourselves.

I am standing before Zeus, staring into the crystal sphere. For the first time, I notice that the sphere no longer appears crystalized, but soft and malleable.

"May I touch the sphere?" I ask.

He nods, and I reach out with one finger. As I suspect, the sphere is yielding, like a warm sponge, yet it looks as clear as any crystal I have ever seen.

"How is that possible?" I ask.

Zeus shrugs, obviously not wanting to give a long explanation. "Although when in a physical form crystals are, indeed, crystalline, in other realms they may embody the properties that a three-dimensional crystal can only contain in essence."

He looks at me challengingly. "Would you now like to experience the Tom who did *not* change—the Tom who was unable to express his possibilities?"

I am puzzled by his remark. "But he did live his potential. Or at least, I did, and he and I are One."

"This is true, but there is a probable Tom who did not. All human life is probabilities, because you have free will and choice." He chuckles grimly. "Even the nonchoice of fear. You may experience that probability if you wish."

"I don't wish!" I say vehemently. "I had enough of that aspect of Tom when I first experienced him/me. Besides, I like happy endings," I say lamely.

Zeus had known I would not want the negative experience, for he is already indicating that I should speak with the man who, I think, was Thor. I thank Zeus, and walk across to Thor. As I reach him, the purple light seems to billow up around my body, recharging me with energy and vitality.

"Are—er, were you Thor?" I ask

He looks very young, and unlike my past image of Thor, he is ash blond. His eyes are a pale gray, very direct, and somehow reassuring.

"To be clear with you, Michael, I embodied Thor for your benefit, but I am not Thor. Bearing this in mind, and knowing your need to identify us in some way, you may call me Thor. However, in keeping with the way you identify me as a God of war, I offer you an experience of you in battle. This is my gift to you."

Horrors! What a gift!

Thor laughs, easily hearing my thoughts. "Don't worry. I *am* offering you a gift, not a senseless fight. There are many wonderful experiences and gifts to be found in battle. You must surely realize that there are many battlefields on Earth; some are within a marriage, some involve a whole neighborhood, some are even called sport, but seldom are they recognized as war zones. However, when you are consciously in a battle, and you believe that you are fighting for survival or justice, you may question the truth of just what it is that you are really fighting for."

I was puzzled by his enigmatic remark. "I don't really understand what you mean."

Thor looks at me directly. "I offer you the experience, not an explanation."

Knowing now that I am safe in these experiences, no matter what the circumstances, I agree.

He, too, holds a crystal sphere in his hand, an entrance through the Gates of Time. Knowing the routine, I peer into the sphere, and . . .

. . . I am a Roman soldier, dressed in full armor. I am saturated in sweat, immersed in a stream of stink. My name is Lucius, and I am eighteen years of age. I am in a bloody war, and I know not why I fight. I know only that my enemies are the Etruscans. Why they are my enemy I have no real understanding. I do know that I am going to die. Word has reached me that we are winning the battle, but our enemies do not seem to know this. I am in the thick of a hand-to-hand fight, and although I am trained to kill, and skillful at it, I am bone weary. I hardly have the strength to lift my sword, and sweat runs into my eyes, blinding me. Through my tortured lungs, I inhale the sweet smell of warm blood, intermingled with the stink of human excreta as bowels are violently emptied in pain and death. It is seldom spoken about, but we soldiers have to piss on ourselves to relieve our bladders as we fight. We stink dreadfully, yet I can smell acrid vomit intermixed with the unmistakable smell of death. Why do my senses seem to be more acute when I slash and hack at other men? Ugh! I am deeply cut across my arm, and the end is very close.

Suddenly, it seems that I am alone with one other man, an enemy. He, too, is young, and I smell his fear like my own. We cut and thrust at each other, yet I sense that he also has no heart for this fight. He is a victim of war as much as I. He slips on the entrails of a dead man, and I am poised to thrust my sword deep into his belly. His eyes, stark with a terrible dread, lock with mine, and I pause. I have no wish to kill him, but I must if I am to survive.

I have hesitated too long. He recovers his balance and hacks at my neck. Surprisingly, there is very little pain. I feel a gush of blood, and, as my energy ebbs, I sink to the gory, bloodied earth. My enemy lowers his sword, staring at me with a look of utter defeat. I see pity in his eyes. It is his last mistake. He, too, is dying. There is no respite on the battlefield. In the brief moment he offered me pity, he has been fatally wounded. He collapses beside me, and we lie together, our faces almost touching as we regard each other. With the last of my strength, I smile at him. I have no hate, no anger, no rage. As my eyes glaze over, I see him smiling back before his face goes slack and empty.

What is happening? This is incredible. He and I are standing on the battlefield, our hands clapsed. Nobody sees us, and although the battle rages around us, we are excluded. I am amazed to see a glorious angel standing next to me, and another with my friend. I realize now that he is a friend, a dear friend. I am puzzled. Why were we fighting each other? Instead of answers, the angel near me embraces me, its huge white wings of light folding around me, and I am lifted.

I am lying on a bed in a cool room. I am not alone. In another bed alongside me is the young man who killed me. He is watching me.

"Hail, Pavron," he says.

"Cedrus! What is happening? Where are we?" I cry out.

"Are you angry that I killed you?" he asks.

"Oh Gods, no! I am thankful," I gasp. "My life was the worst life possible. But, but how do I know this?"

The angel who had enfolded me comes into my view. It walks over to me, and laying a hand on my brow, it puts me into a trance. In my trance, I see real-life pictures, where I am able to access several other of my life cycles.

I watch other battles, recognizing Cedrus and me on the same side. I watch us compete, each seeing who could kill the most of our enemy. Had I been again involved, I would have been sick to my stomach, but I knew I was viewing this as an observer. Even so, listening to the frenzied shout of my blood lust, and witnessing my mad desire to kill, I feel nauseated, mortified.

Cedrus and I were inseparable friends under normal conditions; it was only on the battlefield that our rivalry came to the surface. I am deeply ashamed when I see the outcome of this. He and I were fighting, back to back, surrounded by the enemy. I was in a killing rage, trying to outdo Cedrus, for it was said by many that no soldier was more valiant than Cedrus, no man more skilled at fighting.

As we fought, each supporting the other, I became aware that he was, indeed, a better swordsman than I, as one after another fell to his blade. Then I did something appalling. I pretended to slip, while the sword in my outflung arm sliced cleanly through the tendon behind his knee.

I was shocked by my own betrayal. As he fell, Cedrus, perceiving my guilt, swore at me, vowing eternal revenge. He knew it was no accident. Moments later, he was dead, hacked to pieces. I died only minutes later, unsupported by his sword and skill.

I watch as the moving picture reveals a procession of my life cycles following that betrayal. In each life, Cedrus and I fought bitterly. We went through a life of him betraying me, and then one with me murdering him, on and on, one terrible life of hate and revenge after another. And we both became sickened by it.

In the life cycle that has just ended, I held back my sword, and reluctantly, Cedrus killed me. All I could feel was gratitude to him, and enormous love.

The moving picture ends. My eyes are open, and Cedrus is smiling at me. "How ironic that the love and honor we feel for each other should be found through hate," he says.

The angel speaks for the first time. "You have each learned that hate is no more than unrealized Love. You have learned this by experiencing it. In this way, it becomes part of your knowing, your wisdom."

The angel is right. I know that never again will I fight on the battlefield of war, although life will continue to be the battlefield for many more of my lessons.

I am again with Thor, peering into the sphere. I raise my eyes to meet his. "That was not nice," I say, unsuccessfully trying to be flippant.

"No, probably not, but what have you really learned from it?" Thor asks me.

My insight surprises me. "If I review all the battles and fighting in context with the experiences that Zeus gave me of Tom, I see that an overall picture emerges. If we contain hate or anger, or seek revenge over some injustice, then it is this very hate and outrage over something we abhor that creates the battlefields. Our physical wars are a creation of the base negativity that dominates and rules us through our own personal thoughts and emotions.

"This is true of two people having a feud, a mob that is rioting, or a nation of people that hold a hate or grudge toward another nation. No matter if it is one person, or many people, we each create the reality we are currently involved in." I smile brightly. "Do you know that there are men who, having been ordered to fight in some of our more recent wars, have refused to fight, refused to kill. They are generally abused for this, punished, and often victimized, yet the victory is theirs. They have already won their war. This gives me hope. It tells me that change is happening, and that some of us are learning to express a greater love."

Thor nods at me approvingly and turns away.

I wander among these Great Beings for a while, deliberately walking into the purple light, getting recharged and energized. Only as I feel its energy do I realize that my experiences within the spheres are quite demanding. I am participating in a way I do not understand, and I feel fatigue after each encounter.

She whom I knew to be Persephone comes over to me. "Would you like the gift I have to offer?"

She holds her sphere before me. I am sure her offering will not be a painful one.

Her face is serious. "Knowing that you make your own pain, could you not have an experience without it?"

Her comment opens up a new line of thought. "Do you mean that the me that is here, now, can influence the identity of my past? I did not realize that."

Persephone laughs merrily. "Who do you think Tom, the crofter, saw in his dream if it was not the you of now? Who do you think entered Romany's dream and told her of her past, if it was not you?"

"But . . . but I know nothing of her past. And how could I tell her that when I was Tom? Equally, how could I be in his dream?" I am bewildered all over again.

"Michael, can you believe me when I tell you that as a participant, you acted? You played out your Tom role, but you, who are also Michael, were also involved. On other levels of Self, you acted, bringing a solution into the lives of those you were involved with. You were able to do this because of the paradox of time. What *was* happening or *will* happen *is* happening now. Because of this, the past and the future are always accessible in the present moment. You accessed the past, and brought about change. Only you could do this. I don't have permission to alter your life; neither does anyone else."

I am flabbergasted. "You mean it was I who brought myself into this mystical realm?" I ask weakly.

"But of course. Who else could? However, you may well have a guiding mentor, even if unseen. Even so, all that you are involved in is your choice. It is in your reality because of that choice."

Persephone held up a familiar sphere. "Would you like to experience my gift to you?"

This time I did not hesitate. "Yes, please," I say, my eyes already staring into the sphere.

I am a farmer, walking across my field of wheat. My hands are clasped behind my back, my head down, my eyes on the fresh green blades as I walk across the field. I love what I am doing. To see the young wheat, having just emerged through the soil, is a blessing that I enjoy every season.

The autumn wind is cool now, and the wheat will not grow fast. It will grow stronger and root deeply; then, when the cold of winter comes, and frost and snow take hold of the soil, the wheat will wait with the infinite patience of all plants for the warmth of spring. And then it will begin to grow again.

My footsteps are deliberately slow, prolonging the pleasure of being with the wheat. Some of the neighboring farmers smile when they see me. "There goes old Bert," they say, "walking his fields in his usual dream." None of them has ever been able to understand my depth of feeling for the land. They talk of loving the land, but love is not words. Loving the land is communing with its spirit, sharing its mysteries.

In our mid-nineteenth century England, farming is a hard, labor-intensive way of life, demanding in its hours of work, but I love it. My beloved wife, Poll, understands and honors me for the way I am, but my sons have mixed feelings about me.

My thoughts dwell on my sons as I walk the soothing fields, my feet finding their unerring way across the land. Charlie has a feel for the land and has farmed with me for a good many years now, but Joe is a stranger to it. Charlie will be the one to inherit my land, for Joe has no interest in it at all. Pity, I muse; I had high hopes for Joe. Ah well, doctoring is a worthy thing to do, and he is a mighty fine doctor, but he will never experience my connection with the land. But, then, neither will Charlie. He has a feel for the land, but it is outside of him. He thinks I'm mad when I tell him that I am the land. I feel the movement of the soil in the depths of my own body, and I can hear the Spirit of the Land as it speaks to me. That's what eludes Charlie. Not only doesn't he hear it, but he doesn't believe that it's possible.

I sigh. I am getting old. Approaching ninety, I am at the end of my active life, but I am still able to spend hours walking the land I love.

As I walk the field of wheat, the green blades swirling around me in the breeze, I feel the dance of life in every single plant. I sit for a while in the hedgerow, my back against a sturdy hawthorne. I planted this hedge some sixty years ago. I set it so that the pheasants and partridges would have nesting sites, and so that the ladybirds could find shelter for hibernation. I know that Nature never really attacks my crops; She only protects them.

My eyes closed, I imagine the young wheat growing tall and strong. I marvel at its hollow stem that can always come upright again, no matter how flattened by a storm it may be.

I become still and quiet, without thoughts. I listen, as the Spirit of the Land speaks from the Silence.

"Change is sweeping the planet. This will affect all humanity, but first it will appear in Nature. Species will die, the land will be abused, the water will be polluted and even the air will become unbreathable. This will be seen as a great wrong by humanity, but it is not so. Before there can be a rebirthing, there must be a dying. Having coexisted for a long no-time, the old must give way to the new, for this is the way of life. Those people who are sensitive to the land will be involved in this Change, and you will be the agents for its birth. You will work together, not aware of your togetherness. Some of you will be the destroyers, breaking down the old, while others will be the rebuilders, activating the new. You will see yourselves as opposite in your intent, but you are One. In Oneness, there can be nothing out of place, nothing that is not of the Whole."

I am shocked by what I hear. Species dying, the land abused. I shudder. Maybe it is good that I am old, for I would not wish to witness this terrible change.

Am I demented in my old age? A woman has appeared before me, from nowhere, a woman of great beauty. She is speaking to me.

"You are a wise and gifted farmer, and I honor you, but would you deny the Earth its harvest? For long centuries the Earth has been growing, each century as a moment in the life of your wheat. Would you deny the wheat its yield of grain, the seed that will ensure its continuity? The Earth also has its harvest to reap. Why is this so terrible?"

"Who are you?" I gasp.

"Know me as Persephone, the Goddess of Harvest."

"But this cannot be," I protest. "Persephone is myth, fiction. She is not real or living."

"This may be true, Bert, but is harvest also fiction?"

"I don't know what you mean. I am old and confused."

She smiles at me lovingly. "On the contrary, you are one of the clearest and wisest of your time. Close your eyes, and allow me to show you the harvesting of Earth. Indeed, I shall show you your role within all this, but you must recognize yourself."

I partly close my eyes, peering through the lashes at the beautiful woman before me. She reaches out, her hand touching my brow. Instantly, the lights go out!

I am walking across a field of young wheat. My hands are clasped behind my back in a way that has always been familiar to me. They say even as a boy I walked like this. My eyes are on the fresh green blades, each leaf telling me its story of the growing plant.

It is late twentieth century, and I am an old man. An old stick-in-the-mud some call me. I have watched a century of change in agriculture such as I would never have thought possible, but the feelings in my heart always told me the truth when I was seeking answers to my problems.

My memories take me back to when I was a young man on this same farm. Just down the road, only a few miles from my farm, a new fertilizer factory had opened for business. My heart told me that this new form of fertilizer was not going to be in the long-term interest of us farmers, yet the facts and figures they showed me of yield increases in wheat and barley were mighty impressive. My problem was whether to use it on my own crops or not.

The representative who regularly came to see me was very persuasive, and I don't doubt he believed in the product himself. The crop yields he told me about were so good, so far beyond anything I had ever known, that in the end I succumbed. The glossy, colored illustrations of wheat and barley that appeared so superior to mine were very convincing and persuasive, so I began to use the new fertilizers.

All went well for a time, yet my heart was troubled. I was mixed and muddled for a good many years, trying to combine the chemical fertilizers with an organic approach to the land. My heart held the organic growing principles, but my head was filled with facts about chemical fertilizers. Very soon I had to learn about the chemicals needed to kill weeds and insects and fungi.

For twenty years, I waged war on my farm. Unrealized, my beloved farm had become a battlefield, and the enemy was Nature. How did all my common sense and my innate feeling for the land slip away from me? In my heart, I knew that the weeds and insects that I was spraying with chemicals had never been a problem in the days before chemical fertilizers, but I consoled myself with the huge increase in crop yields. And so it went, year after year, the problems increasing, the profit margin decreasing, and the land getting sicker with each passing season.

I inherited this land from my father, who in turn had inherited it from his father, my grandfather. I was even named Herbert, after him.

I was persuaded to cut down all the hawthorne hedges on my farm—the hedges my grandfather had planted when he was a young man. I don't think he would have been too proud of me for that. I was told that the growing crops would get more light and air and that I would gain several yards more cropping land in each field. To my shame, I ignored the needs of the birds and hedgerow animals, and all the vast array of insects. However, to my credit, twenty years later I planted them again, and I even set other trees in a new and wider hedgerow to create a more complete ecosystem.

Ecosystem! We have invented words today to describe what my granddad simply knew as Nature. From reading his diaries, I know that he would have called an ecosystem the "diversity of One." And how much more enlightening a description!

In hindsight, I guess we have to make mistakes to learn from them. Time becomes experience, and mistakes become lessons. I certainly made my mistakes. As the discord grew between me and my land, so I began to reap a harvest of distress. Everything changed for the worse. Modern science hybridized the wheats and barleys, forcing them into ever higher yields. But to keep them alive and productive, the crops required more and more chemical fertilizers. On and on it went, one error chasing another. This clever new wheat had a solid stem to support the bigger head of grain, but when the storms came, the solid stem snapped, and the wheat lay wet and spoiled on the ground. Sure, the overall yields were higher, but that only served to oversupply the market, while the cost to produce the grain crops of a decreasing quality increased with every passing year.

Other things bothered me. I would spray my wheat and barley with the various recommended sprays, just like the other farmers, becoming increasingly dependent on the government's agricultural advisory system. In the beginning, I sprayed only for weeds, but insects soon became a problem, and then fungi diseases became commonplace. I did not like the chemicals at all, and with good reason. Not far away, a whole family had been found dead. Mother, father, and three children. It was learned that the water in their well was directly contaminated from the liquid draining out of farm chemical cans in a nearby dump. Such a tragedy was the price of progress.

Meanwhile, a whole new generation of farmers had grown up, and, to them, chemical farming was the only normal way to do things. Farm machinery became larger and more aggressive to the land, culminating in the rotovator. This rotating, multibladed monster chewed up the soil, mixing and churning it, slowly but surely fracturing the very structure of the soil itself. This resulted in wind and water erosion as the soil blew away or washed away, and caused problems within the soil profile as it became degraded.

Adversity is a good teacher. Only when things were really grim on the farm did I finally admit that I was frightened. I was frightened of where agriculture was headed, for it seemed to be on a rapid downhill spiral, and only a few of us could see it. I began to educate myself about the land. I learned about the microorganisms of the soil and their needs, and about the oxygen and water requirements of the soil. I learned about the soil minerals, about humus, and about earthworms. I learned about the pH of the soil and about the exchange of soil nutrients. I learned the truth about fertilizing the soil. I learned that the so-called chemical fertilizers are no more than chemical stimulants, a drug for the soil—a drug that eventually destroys the microorganic soil life so necessary for biological transmutations, thereby depleting the overall quality of the soil.

I learned that these harmful chemical stimulants also cause massive complexing of the soil minerals, which in turn cost more in money and effort to redress such self-created problems. I learned that the soil is a living, breathing Whole, and, although tolerant of some abuse, it has a very definite point of collapse. I learned that my own farm was approaching that brink!

I changed. I became what is known as an organic farmer. In truth, this means no more than respecting the life in the soil and nourishing it. Instead of using artificial fertilizers to stimulate the growing crops chemically, I fed and nourished the soil life to create an abundance of humus, knowing that this, in turn, would truly fertilize the crops. To fertilize means to *enrich,* not stimulate!

I pulled my farm back from the brink of collapse, and for a decade I was a figure of ridicule among my farming peers. I found a seed supply of the best of the old types of hollow-stem wheats, and it was never broken by storms again. After a few years, other more aware farmers came to see me and to look at my land. They went away amazed. They had seen a soil seething with earthworms, alive and active. They had seen my crops growing with no sign of insect pests and minimal weeds as a result of minimal cultivation. In many ways, I became a teacher, and in time, many organic farming organizations came into being.

The decades passed, and I prospered, for I needed only enough money to keep my family well cared for and happy, and my land became my support instead of my enemy. Those who had ridiculed me looked on with envy, for my farm was known to be outstanding. It was a model of health and top-quality crops. I was paid premium prices for my crops, which were sold only to whole-food suppliers of quality produce.

But of all the changes I made, the greatest change was in me, for I learned about the Spirit of the Land, and I learned to listen to this storehouse of wisdom. I became a student of Nature—I still am—and my rewards for this are many. The hedgerows are now thick and verdant, complete with fruit and nut trees for the wildlife and special thickets for the animals and ground birds. Trees abound on my farm, and it is a healthy, diverse Whole. Now, my old granddaddy would be mighty proud!

My eyes open, and I stare at Persephone in wonder. "That was surely me," I gasp. "Me, my own grandson?" "Shush, we have not finished yet," she whispers. She touches my brow again, and I am . . .

. . . walking across a field of young wheat. I can hear a Song moving through the stillness of my heart. God! What a Song! Rising and falling as though the very breath of the Earth, I hear the Spirit of the Land as it welcomes us.

I turn to the group of young people with me. "Listen," I tell them. "Cease thinking, get into your heart center, and listen. Listen with your total attention." Together, we continue across the field. It is early in the twenty-second century, and I am a young man. I am said to be a mystic, for I was born with the Silent language of Nature flowing through my heart. There are many very gifted people on this planet, although the gifts have changed in many ways. Genius is no longer based on an intellectual capacity, but on a person's spiritual insight and wisdom.

Much has changed. Agribusiness collapsed in the twenty-first century, and all the ingenuity of genetic manipulation was unable to prevent it. There *is* a natural order behind the basic principles of plant growth, and they can be abused only to a critical point. Nature is, was, and always will be an expression of Spirit. For well over a century, this was ignored, the physical manipulation, domination, and stimulation reaping its final destructive harvest. If you sow discord, you are obliged to harvest distress. However, as was always known, from a negative destructuring there emerges a positive restructuring. Agriculture now embraces a reality based on Oneness. The old had to give way to the new, no matter how hard the old battled for its survival.

I am more of a teacher than a farmer, yet my teaching is really about drawing the innate *knowing* from my pupils, rather than putting much extra knowledge in. With the collapse of the abhorrent human need to dominate, the inherent legacy of our inner dominion is now blossoming as it emerges from the soul.

"Bert! I hear the Song," a girl named Mirel whispers.

I smile at her. Most of my pupils are children, or, to be more accurate, old souls in young bodies. Many of them will soon be far more skilled than I.

I watch her eyes as tears roll down her cheeks. My smile deepens. You cannot listen to the Song and remain unaffected. In the Song is heard the movement of clouds, the whisper of the moisture they contain, the soft susurration of displaced air. One hears the sifting of every particle of soil, the breath of a planet, the deep gurgle of its bowels. The trees knowingly add to the Song, as a breeze strokes across the harp of their leaves, while each bird adds its own expression of joy to the concert of Nature.

Farming is very different now. All farmers—and there are more female than male farmers—are at One with their farm. All farmers are Awake, knowing their Self. Their sense of Self is expanded, embracing their land and everything that lives on their farm. Some have a very expanded sense of Self, some quite small, yet the inner expansion continues. There are no concepts within this. You *know*, or you do not. Within this expanding framework, each farmer controls his or her farm with Love-focused will-power—true dominion. Each farm is fine-tuned with Love, the greatest creative power of all.

All farmers can control the germination and growth of all the plants on their land. They can alter the pH of the soil at will, where they wish it, and control the activity and movement of all the insects. Nothing is outside of Self, and no factor is seen as wrong or right. Even the rainfall responds to the will of the farmer. Harmony and balance are the governing principles, and they can only be expressed from within the farmer who has attained this wholeness. This *is* the dominion of Self.

The old mono-agribusiness has been replaced by a true diversity. The abusive farm chemicals and genetically forced plant varieties have all gone. Farming now is a co-hesion of peace and abundance, reflecting the peace and abundance within the farmer. These are the criteria that determine who can have the privilege of farming, for it is now considered a distinction to be a custodian of the land. Those who can attune with the Spirit of the Land are honored.

I catch the eye of Mirel, and she grins at me, the delight breaking out into laughter. She is eleven years old in body, but I already recognize that she has greatness in her aura. I am honored that I am teaching a person who will become one of the great teachers of our time.

Time! Of all the changes, time is the most changed. Life

is measured now by a vibrational intensity, rather than the measure of a clock. In body, I am a young man, yet I am dying. I have dreamed my death, and I welcome it. I have seen into the Beyond, and it is open to me, offering me a new direction within other dimensions. My friends know of this, and they rejoice with me. My death will not be an ending; it will be a new beginning.

Mirel is looking at me strangely. She comes to me, taking my hand. "Bert, your light is shining more powerfully than I have ever seen. Are you leaving us?"

I realize that she is correct. My sense of Self is now vast, expanding far beyond the capacity of my physical body. I feel the physical shell fall away, and I am free.

The light is so powerful around me that even Persephone is bathed in my radiance. My eyes open, and I nod as she beckons to me. Rising to my feet, I walk toward her. On a sudden premonition, I turn around, and I see my body— old Bert—slumped and empty as he leans back against the hawthorn, an expression of deep peace stamped on his lined and weathered features.

Taking Persephone's hand, I walk with her into other dimensions, knowing that she is a messenger of light.

I step back from the sphere, shaken. For moments I am confused, having connected so strongly with the three lives of Bert. I am a bit stunned at how it ended.

"He died! Or was reborn. Whew!"

Persephone regards me intently. "How do you feel about all that? I must say, I am surprised."

"You are surprised!" I am startled. "But didn't you arrange everything? Wasn't this the lesson you wanted me to learn?"

"Michael, don't you understand yet? We do not organize what you experience; *you* do. The people you experience are not separate from you. You go where Self reveals Self. Each person whom you experience is an aspect of Self. *You* choose, *you* determine, because it is *you* that *you* experience."

My head is spinning, but within my heart an inner knowing is ignited. I don't intellectually understand, but within me, I know that I know!

Leaving me to digest all that has happened, Persephone moves away. I deliberately walk into the purple mist that billows in small clouds around me. It is odd, but just when I need the purple light, it always seems to surge close by. Very nice! It is so energizing, but more than that, the purple mist seems to dispel my confusion, promoting a greater clarity and insight.

I am approached by a tall man who is absolutely startling to look at. I see an incredible, almost ethereal beauty in him, as though his garment of a human body is not quite adequate to hide the intense and magnificent energy. I feel certain that this is Pan, even though he looks nothing like the mythological Pan as depicted by the books of my youth. As though to mock me, tiny stub horns seem to momentarily gleam at his brow; then they are gone.

I feel more music around him and somehow a greater affinity with him than with any of the others. He attracts me while simultaneously overwhelming me. He stands quiet and patient, knowing that his presence is disturbing me.

"Do you remember me?" he asks.

I gasp. Not his words but his energy is invoking some powerful memories of my youthful past. In experiences that I dismissed as daydreams, I was led into the mystical realms of Nature. There, I experienced depths and perceptions of Nature that I could never explain, so I persuaded myself they were foolish dreams. I know, now, they were not.

For a micromoment, the mask of Pan slips, and I sense a wilderness in human garb. I sense Nature unbounded by human thought, undiluted by human concepts. I sense something that is nameless, formless, and indescribable.

I swallow nervously, for Pan holds his sphere before me.

His enigmatic half smile is a question.

Suddenly, as though compelled, my hesitation is banished, and I thrill with all that is happening. I know that when I eventually return to a normal, everyday reality, I will not be the same as before. This whole experience is an initiation.

With avid attention, I gaze deep into his sphere.

My name is Mirel, and with my three children, I am walking in the woods. Laurel and Fey, young teenagers, dance ahead, skipping through the autumn leaves, but my youngest, five-year-old Bert, walks with me, holding my hand.

"Come on, Mummy," Laurel calls out silently, impatient, and I call back to her in the Silence.

"We are coming, my dear. Don't go too far ahead."

In the Silence, I hear her reply. "Okay."

I am not sure if I am teaching young Bert, as we walk along together, or if he is teaching me. I named him after an honored teacher in my youth. I was with my teacher, Bert, when he became so illumined that he left his physical body, forsaking it. It was both a sad and exultant moment in my life. Bert actually manifested himself before me in his new light body, for unlike a normal human light body, it was radiant beyond belief. He spoke to me, telling me that he was going Beyond, and that I would eventually join him. He told me that we are soul-bonded.

Young Bert—everyone calls him "young Bert"—is an amazing child. Like most of us, he perceives the Nature Spirits, but he can also perceive a dimension beyond this. He can see into a dimension of Beings that occupy the same space as us, but they express a very different reality. Their vibrational intensity is far higher than the physical manifestation of Nature and humanity. Young Bert tells me that they appear as reflections of Light, without any defined form. They communicate not with words, but with a beautiful kaleidoscope of spherical light frequencies. I know what he means, but I have never experienced anything quite like it. He cannot join them, but, nevertheless, they are able to teach him, taping directly into his consciousness.

As he and I walk into the Clearing, Fey and Laurel are waiting for us. "The Empress is expecting us," Laurel says in a hushed tone. Young Bert is literally twitching with excitement. The Clearing is thickly carpeted with yellow and gold leaves falling softly from the surrounding trees. As though by magic, the subdued light picks up and reflects the multihued colors of autumn, while all around us the trees are hushed. The Clearing is a place of power. It is a place where the visible and the invisible mix and merge, where the form and the formless no longer appear as separate. Not all humans are able to discern these places of power, but most can, especially those who work directly with Nature. For us, this merging is necessary. The Clearing is bordered by the trees, tightly packed as though jostling for room. It is not a large Clearing, no bigger than an old-fashioned tennis court, but it holds far more than its physical space would suggest.

Together, we all walk over to what appears as an archway of light, walking beneath the shimmering portal. As we enter the archway, we walk into a pink light that is so dense it appears almost solid. We have to push against its formless resistance as though facing a powerful, unmoving wind. It's a strange feeling. Most people are unable to penetrate this pink intensity and are therefore denied entry beneath the archway. My children and I have all been here before, so I know that all will go well for us.

I remember back to when I first brought each of the children here. They were all three-month-old babes in arms when I carried them through the archway and presented them to the Empress. The Empress was delighted. Only a few people are able to enter her kingdom, and to have a whole family is quite an exception. What makes my family exceptional is that each of my children has a different father. I have never pledged myself to any one man, but with each of the three men whom I love, I have borne a child. This was my choice. Laurel is my firstborn. She can speak into the Silence of the Self more clearly than anyone I have known and already is in demand as a teacher. She can teach on the inner levels over any distance, making her invaluable.

Fey is my second born. She is Fey by name and fey by nature. She can see Nature Spirits of all types, and she can easily communicate with them. She has a very developed affinity with Nature, and she is working in new levels of horticulture.

And then there is young Bert. He is an odd child. He seemed almost retarded for his first year of life, but we eventually realized that he was in touch with so many other realities that he paid little attention to his physical one. He is now well adjusted, but he has never attended the schools of other children. Even though our schools are very versatile, catering to the varied degrees of brain-hemisphere development, young Bert seemed already to know just about everything. He never told us about this, but it became apparent as he was tested and assessed.

I have to confess, that I, too, am considered a person on the forefront of human development, but I am not in any way an intellectual. I specialize in the areas of metaphysical integration with other realms of reality.

The pink intensity offers its usual impenetrable resistance before suddenly melting before us, and we enter the realm of Nature Spirits. As always, the Empress is waiting. Without exception, she knows when a human seeks entry to her kingdom.

"Welcome." Her voice is silent, emerging directly into our human consciousness. Her smile of love is uplifting, a song in the heart.

"Thank you, Empress," we each silently project.

I have learned that we humans each see the Empress in a different way. Some share a similar perception of her, but I know that how we see her is our own creation. I am aware that young Bert sees her with his inner eye as a moving, mobile spectrum of Light, reflecting through colors and frequencies invisible to normal human eyes. For him, she is one of the Beings who teach him. Perhaps his perception is more accurate than mine, but it matters not at all. To Laurel, the Empress is a feminine figure of brilliant white Light, while to Fey she is a fairy Being of exceptional beauty.

I see her as feminine and human, yet with a visible aura and a magnificent rippling corona around her head. This is the way most human adults see her, and it is that luminous halo radiating like a regal crown that has brought about the title of Empress.

Joining her energy with ours, she accompanies us as we continue our stroll. In some ways, everything has changed; in other ways, it is all the same. The archway in the mystic Clearing is the portal through which to pass into this other realm, but the realm occupies the same space as our physical realm. The trees still grow around us, but these trees seem to manifest a different level of awareness. They communicate with us, even to the extent that leaves give excited little dances around their stems, and twigs twitch toward us, all aware of our presence and welcoming our attention. The same trees grow in our physical reality, but our physical senses are in a slower vibration, dulling our Greater Reality. When I was a girl, my teacher, Bert, opened me to the Song. I have since become proficient at listening, able to summon the required attention and focus necessary to inner-hear the Song in a physical reality. Here, however, the Song is almost overpowering. It fills my whole Being, opening me to a greater experience of life than is physically possible. The Song is pure energy in movement.

Holding hands with my children, we kick up our heels and dance to the harmonics of the Song, and, in consciousness, the trees dance with us. And they love it!

We dance with fairies and gnomes and elves as they all come in a rush and flood of eager awareness from within the wood. I join hands with a group of laughing fauns, each looking as though an ancient child. We whirl and spin, no longer with our feet on the earth, as we float a few feet above ground. For what seems hours we dance an inexhaustible dance of Love, and we are aware that our energy is permeating and nourishing the consciousness of all Nature.

This incredible kingdom, where the Empress serves the realms of the physical and the metaphysical, is a meeting place between the two aspects of a Greater Reality. Here, the two aspects of One come together, thus raising forever the vibration of physical life on a physical Earth. Within our joy, and within our dance, we are focused and aware. Within us, the Song is expanded and amplified, and its influence over humanity becomes increasingly magnified.

Not only do we magnify the Song, attracting it to human awareness, but we open human awareness to the energy of the Song. We express the Song of Truth, thus increasing the resonance of Truth within everyday human lives. This joy is our service.

7

The Pillar of Green Light

Understanding is not always appropriate
for it attempts to rationalize true Mystery.
Mystery is Truth unrealized.
Understanding is based on Truth
that has been rationalized, but not realized.

I stare up at Pan, but he is not to be seen. Neither he nor his sphere is anywhere near me. I glance around, puzzled. I don't understand. How could I return from the sphere if it is not here? More Mystery. Forget it, Michael.

Mirel! What an incredible life. What an amazing family! Was she me, of the future? I smile. Forget it. Put aside questions and live the Mystery.

Glancing around, I realize that the Great Beings are indirectly observing me. Within me, I feel the birth of a great joy—a deep inner knowing that all life is as it should be. No matter how much I do or do not know, there are other Beings involved in the outworkings of Mother Earth and her marvelous Nature, as well as in the torturous expressions of humanity. We are not alone, not abandoned. Suddenly, a duality of seeing takes place. I can see the Great Beings around me, but equally, in the same space, I have a vision of another time on a future/now Earth. I see a rich, green Earth filled with teeming wildlife, but there are birds and animals that are new to me.

As my vision expands, becoming stronger, an inner knowing accompanies it. I know that in my present time/frame, where Nature seems to be under threat as species die, becoming extinct to us, other species that have not yet taken on physical form are already being held within the creative consciousness of rebirth. These other animals and birds are in a formless state of manifestation, and not until the moment is ripe will they take on physical form.

Now, in my vision, I see resplendent birds that express new qualities in the bird kingdom. I see colors that I cannot identify, and I sense perceptual abilities in the birds that are new to their expression. I see animals that are different, but, again, the difference is not so much in form as in their qualities of expression. These animals are more advanced in their intelligence, more capable of a partner relationship with humans than most animals of our present time. Today we own our animals, but within this vision I sense a real partnership, not ownership. By attempting to own them, inadvertently, we would once again express our domination and separateness, and this future is of unity, not separation.

I see many species of trees that have long been extinct growing and flourishing in their climatic zones. There are even trees from a time/frame before this; trees that will be heralded as new species, even though they are not. Part of me is in awe, astonished by the resources of Nature, but a vastly older, wiser Self knows that within the greater frame of Reality that is Oneness, all is possible within the eternal moment. *Consciousness is never extinct!*

I see a humanity free from the restrictive bonds of hate and of greed. I see peace, true peace. In our present time, the closest we get to peace is trying to resolve conflict. This is not peace. Even the absence of war in society is not peace; peace is the absence of any trace of malice within each person. Peace is an experience of the soul, not an intellectual statement of nonconflict. Peace cannot be experienced by the mind; it can only be witnessed by the mind as the soul Self—who we are—experiences Unconditional Love.

I see groups of people walking through a forest, excited and aware as they perceive the Nature Spirits who surround them. I watch both children and adults as they dance with fauns and elves, scattering the fallen leaves and setting the forest alight with the joy of their shrieks of delight. True joy is a resonance that nourishes all life, for true joy cannot be restricted or personalized. Joy is an energy of truth that echoes and resonates throughout all life. This more enlightened humanity has learned that we are the amplifiers of joy, and it is we who uplift the conscious expressions of life on Earth. This is a joy that creates joy, an elevation of spirit.

So overwhelmed am I by the clarity and power of my vision, that I, too, am leaping up and down, cavorting in an abandoned leaping and shrieking of great glee. Grabbing Persephone in a casual way that would have appalled me earlier, we dance and whirl around the Gates of Time, squealing aloud with laughter. With no surprise, I notice that the other Great Beings are also leaping around with incredible whirling grace, not limited to keeping their feet on the ground.

As we dance and whirl in a universal celebration of life, the purple mist is gradually thickening, enshrouding and revitalizing me. Denser and denser it becomes, and the Great Beings are gradually fading, as though being absorbed by the purple fog. The enormous Gates of Time are also becoming faint and nebulous, wavering as though a shimmering mirage until, as the fog arises above me, I cannot see anything or anybody.

Wisp by wisp, the purple mist dissipates, and the Great Beings have vanished. The Gates of Time have gone. Sadly, I stand alone. A faint but resounding echo whispers through the ethers, as though echoing the finality of the vast Gates of Time. I am standing in the area that was once a living City, becoming in turn the playground of our ancient mythological Gods and Goddesses.

I am puzzled. Was all that happened another strange manifestation created by the Light of Enlightenment? I sigh. No answers as usual. Ah well, back to Mystery.

Once again I walk to the crest of the hill, glancing back continually to see if any more miraculous manifestations are about to take place. The lagoon of liquid light is just as before, but something has changed, and I realize what it is. The sun is setting. Is that possible? Can day ever die in this mystical realm? Is time even measured in days? Is there any time to measure? With my questions comes a clear realization: This truly is a timeless realm. A day is a concept here; there is no time.

As I stare up at the sun, willing it to shine with its friendly pink light and inner warmth, I realize that it is not setting, for it is still high in the sky, but it is fading. How can a sun fade out while high in the sky? I watch, and it seems that the heavens have gone mad, for the sky is rapidly changing to a deep burgundy red, yet with a clarity that removes any trace of threat. I am aware that I would not want a dark night in this reality, but even as I think it, I know that this place is an expression of Light, that there can be no darkness here.

This timeless realm is weird, to put it mildly. How will I ever be able to share my experiences with my friends. Only Treenie will know I am not crazy. I am only too aware of how I fear being ridiculed. I am convinced that I have been ridiculed and persecuted in other lives, but I also feel a reassurance that this will not happen again. All that is required is that I share my experience and Truth with the people for whom it is perfect timing. Truth always remains a Truth, but only within a person's perfect timing can Truth be recognized and accepted.

Of Treenie's timing for Truth there can be no doubt. Even if she does not remember being with me in her dream state, she will accept my experiences with far more ease than I will be able to. Treenie has always been that way. She walks her path with serenity, while I stumble along. To be fair to me, however, Treenie does not have experiences like this to deal with. How did I get into something like this? How can I be physically sitting in bed, diligently scribbling this down in a poetic form, while at the same time be in a light body experiencing a timeless realm of Mystery? I sigh. I will need all the support from Treenie I can get when I am back in a physical reality.

Watching the burgundy sky, I notice that it is still changing. The red is slowly melting away, leaving the sky as the deepest of pinks, but even more strange, the sky is rippling! Like a fast-flowing river over a bed of rocks, the sky is a rippling ocean of pink, both a wonder and, oddly enough, exhilarating. Will the strangeness never stop? The bizarre effect of a rippling sky of pink is reflected onto the ground. All around me the Nature of this mystic place is wavering, creating in me a feeling of insecurity and uncertainty. Even standing is becoming difficult, for I am feeling increasingly dizzy. This is too much. With a sigh of exasperation, I sit down, my eyes closing, trying for a while to shut it all out. After a timeless moment, an odd feeling sweeps over me. Once again I feel that I am not alone, but when I peek between my fingers to see if I can see someone, or something, there is nothing.

The scenery around me continues to reflect the wavering ripples of the sky, and I feel oddly displaced. I get the peculiar feeling that it is I who am strange, in a place of normality. With increasing intensity, I feel that it is I who am the oddity, while everything else conforms to its own set of rules. Overpoweringly, I want to go home. As I focus on home, I visualize a vast orange sun that fills the sky with a warm, ambient light, and I see the familiar beautiful, slender, lithe Beings of translucent blue. I sense a deep compassion and love waiting for me, whenever I care to return. I know that in the not too distant future I will go home—home to my family on countless stars.

I shake my head in confusion. Wait! That's not home. Where is that place? Who are those Beings? As the powerful memory swiftly fades, I feel a sense of loss so great I choke in despair, stretching out full length on the hilltop as my overwrought emotions cry out for release. Strangely, while I am crying, I again feel that I am not alone. It is as though my tears have washed away a huge dam that has long been built up within me, a dam that has held me away from some deep inner knowing. I know that there is no one with me, yet I am not alone. What this means I do not know, nor do I feel any need to understand it; the inner certainty is enough.

Eventually, my emotions drained, I stand up. How it has happened or what it involves I'm not sure, but some very long-term inner issue has been resolved within me.

For the first time, I feel my own Lightness of Being. Previously, other Beings and outer circumstances have instigated this joy, but this time it comes from some nameless dimension within myself. This is based in who I Am, and while I suspect it will fade, I am certain that it is always within me, waiting to be permanently owned.

Looking up at the sky again, I notice that the change has continued. No longer rippling, the sky is now a deep rich pink, satin smooth in tone and appearance. I get the feeling that the rippling effect was especially for me, for in some mystic way it reached into a long retained, hidden, inner block, igniting memories that I do not understand, yet memories that needed to be released.

Has some cosmic switch been activated? Suddenly, the pink sky is filled with twinkling stars and hurtling planets, unlike anything that I have ever seen, yet it evokes a wondrous and familiar memory. I stare in awe, mesmerized, when I hear a rich, deep voice whisper in Latin.

I whirl around, for it is a human voice, yet there is no one to be seen. The whisper seems to be in my head, and the words—"Semper secundum ordinem"—are utterly meaningless. And then they are not, for in my heart a clear translation emerges: Always according to order. With the translation, an unrealized inner knowing grows to maturity, and like a flower bud, unfolds its truth.

This is about humanity. While it may appear that we humans are jeopardizing the planet Earth, and all the Nature upon it, nothing could be further from the truth. Each star, each heavenly body, has its own life path, its own reality, its own destiny, and we cannot interfere. We can only affect our own reality, our own life path. Only those people who live within a consensus reality can affect the lives of others—the people who adhere to the same beliefs, the same falsity, the same fears, the same illusions.

Within my knowing, I see that everything is in perfect order. We have the power of creation, and creation can destruct, but it can never destroy. The difference is subtle yet immense. Destructuring is the pathway to restructuring, an act of creation based on continuity. We can destroy what we physically build, but what we build is an expression of our consciousness at that time. A building can be destroyed, but only when consciousness is ready to release that expression. We are blinded to this truth by our unfailing mental and emotional attachments, and an unflagging belief in endings and injustice. The movement of the moment sweeps all before it, with or without our permission or understanding!

The immensity of my insight holds me enthralled. No

race of Beings, either human or alien, can take apart the fabric of creation. All so-called destruction is timed to happen only when consciousness is ready to release that form. This applies to biological *and* engineered, constructed forms. For a timeless moment, I stand entranced, my inner realization expanding and blossoming. I am convinced that there is a timing to all that is happening to me. Each new experience seems to peel away another layer of illusion, revealing ever greater clarity and insight.

Because of this, I am not particularly surprised when a bright golden glow appears in the sky, in micromoments traveling from being a speck on the distant horizon to becoming a huge golden globe hovering before me. What does surprise me is that this golden globe appears similar to the Golden Orb I had earlier seen on the topmost spire of the city of living glass. If it isn't the same, it is identical. The last time it had unfolded great petals like some immense flower, revealing a vast interior.

This time, it is rather different. A single petal gently unfolds, swinging down to the ground as though intended to be a ramp. From the interior there comes a deep, rich voice, a voice that I instantly recognize.

"My child, we need you. Please come with me. You know we mean you no harm."

I feel no fear at all—not even a qualm of anxiety or apprehension. Maybe my adventures have been preparing me for this, but this invitation seems so natural and intended I get the feeling that I have been waiting all my life for this very moment.

I walk up the golden ramp into a craft that is so silvery

bright I have to squint and allow my eyes to adjust. As they do, I realize that physical vision could not deal with this brightness; it would be almost blinding. With my eyes comfortable, I gaze around. The interior is spacious, even if not very large, and it seems to have remarkably little gadgetry in it. As I turn around, looking at all that surrounds me, I see the owner of the voice.

Standing within a nimbus of soft white light, an immeasurably ancient man faces me. He is dressed in a long robe and holds a shepherd's staff with a deeply curved crook. I stare in consternation. A shepherd?

"Please feel welcome. Some of your many questions deserve an answer, and there is more I would have you experience."

He stands before me, radiating incredible love and infallible trust. So illumined is he that I can see the nimbus of his radiance. This man invokes the deepest aspects of Love and trust in me, while his wisdom is a force of pure vibration. His ancientness is not something that is manifest in his appearance, but is a feeling I get from his aura.

On a surge of insight, I realize that here, at last, I face the author of my journey, the unseen Shepherd of my adventure. "It was you, wasn't it?" I ask. "It was your voice that whispered to me, and it was you who made all this possible for me. You have been my unseen guide."

"Yes, I did whisper into your heart, and I also precipitated your experiences in this timeless realm, but it was you who made it all possible. Come, let us have a little chat while we travel."

I realize that the petal-like ramp has folded back into

place, and that a faint, subtle vibration is evident. "Where are we?" I ask, a faint quaver to my voice.

"To be exact, 'where' is not the operative word," the Shepherd replies. "'Where' does not apply to this reality. We are not transversing space as you know it, but in truth we are unfolding through frames of reality. I ask only for your trust."

"You know I trust you," I reply. "I'm pretty well certain that you are the guide who has been a major influence in my life for a very long time."

He smiles. "Yes, I have, but in many a different guise. I suppose the next question is to ask for my name."

I nod.

"I have had many names and identities, but who I am is none of these." He frowns thoughtfully. "Know me simply as the Shepherd. This will avoid confusion based on your past or on unnecessary feelings of reverence."

I stare into his serene blue eyes. A deep, startling king-fisher blue, his eyes speak of the most profound wisdom and compassion. Just staring into those eyes renews and uplifts me.

With one hand on my shoulder, he guides me through an open doorway into another part of the craft. This golden globe is as deceptive as the Golden Orb of the city, for we are now in a long, wide corridor, with many doors leading into other rooms all along it. I suspect that what I saw as a golden globe in reality may be something quite different. The Shepherd steers me into an average-size room, comfortably furnished in a human style, and bids me to be seated.

I sit back with a deep relaxing sigh, while questions bubble to the surface of my mind.

The Shepherd holds up his hand. "Wait. Let me explain first, and then I will answer any remaining questions." He sits back, relaxing, and softly claps his hands together. Immediately, a shaft of pink light beams onto me, bathing me in nourishment. I feel myself absorbing this pink light into my light body with all the relief of a physically thirsty person gulping down much needed water.

"I didn't know I so needed that!"

"You could hardly be expected to know. You are much more familiar with your physical body than with your light body."

He smiles at me, engaging and friendly. "You are a normal, mortal, human Being in this life span, yet, like all other people, you are also an immortal Being of Light. You, Michael, are a very old soul." He waves his arms in an all-encompassing gesture of space and life. "You have been around."

A question leaps to my mind, but he holds up a hand to forestall it.

"I am not going into long explanations, because *you* are going to discover your own truth. That is the reason behind this exercise—to give you a deeper insight into the many dimensions of Self. When you Awaken to the truth of Self, then your purpose on planet Earth will unfold. This metaphysical experience is happening because you have willed it so. These timeless realms that you are exploring and discovering are part of a Greater Reality. Life is not all transient and physical, nor is it all bound by physical law. As an old soul, your inner truth can no longer be denied. Your Lightness of Being demands that you Awaken to a Greater Reality and that you fulfill your purpose."

Questions that had clamored for my attention die.

The Shepherd looks me in the eyes. "Like a caterpillar that has reached the timing of its butterfly self, so you are close to the timing of your greater Self. Just as the caterpillar in its cocoon experiences the titanic forces of change, so these same forces will rip apart the fabric of life as you perceive it. How long you stay in the destructuring cycle of the cocoon is up to you. This is not being thrust upon you; it is your choice, your reason in taking physical incarnation on Earth."

Even though this does not answer all my questions, it is enough. I realize that my questions need their answers lived, not explained. However, I do have one last question.

"I get the feeling you could appear to me in any way that you wish. Why as a shepherd?"

"I wish to powerfully imprint the image of a Shepherd into your consciousness."

"But why?"

The Shepherd smiles gently, his face expressing concern. "Because it is symbolic of an inner Truth that you contain, with all its attendant responsibilities. You will deny this, of course. In fact, you will more than deny it; you will fight against it." He smiles encouragingly. "That is one reason why you are here now."

I feel disconcerted, for I am very aware of my instant denial of his words. I don't even want to discuss it.

"You say that is one reason I am here. Is there another reason?"

"Yes. You are discovering that your long suppressed metaphysical self is very powerful. Your logical/physical self has been dominant until now, but this Greater Reality is revealing another aspect of Self. It is appropriate, now, for your metaphysical Self to move into ascendency."

I stare at the Shepherd thoughtfully. What he is saying makes sense. Until now, I have suppressed my metaphysical experiences, mainly because of the fear of being different. But I am enjoying the wonder of this timeless realm and the insights and capacities it is revealing in me.

"Where are we going?" I ask. "Are we leaving Earth? In fact, where is the place I have just come from?"

The Shepherd smiles patiently. "Your question mode is still in gear. However, I agree, some explanation is in order. We are not really going to a place, or places. As I said earlier, we are moving through frames of reality. Your three-dimensional, physical Earth plane is a reality zone. We are no longer in that same zone; therefore, we are in a different continuum, but we have not traveled any place to do this."

"I really don't understand you."

The Shepherd shrugs. "To put it in the simplest possible terms, you are a Being of Light. This is your Greater Reality. When your consciousness of Self focuses on your Light Beingness, then you experience a greater, metaphysical Reality, and your reality expands into other realms, or frames of experiential reference. This is what is happening to you now. When your consciousness focuses only through your physical self, then you only experience your everyday, physical reality. Both are true, yet the physical reality contains definite limits, while a metaphysical Reality takes you beyond them. Believing only in a physical reality maintains those limitations."

"Hmmmm. I think I get it. It is as though life as I physically know it is a consensus reality of soap and water in a bubble pipe. When you blow into the pipe, the soap and water form a bubble, which gradually expands. In essence, it is all the same substance, yet the bubble expands into new dimensions of expression, extending far beyond the consensus reality of mere soap and water."

The Shepherd laughs and claps his hands in delight. "An excellent metaphor. I could not have put it better myself."

Jumping to his feet, he heads out the door, beckoning to me. "Come on. You have a few friends wanting to meet you again."

I follow him down the wide corridor. Friends? What friends? What is he talking about? The farther we walk down the corridor, the longer it seems to become. Suddenly, the Shepherd flings open a door and ushers me in. "I'll see you later," he says in a soft voice and whisks back out the door, closing it behind him.

Apprehensive, I gaze around me. I am no longer in a room, but in a soft twilight landscape of sand and low dunes. A feeling of peace pervades the atmosphere and, despite this being so startlingly unexpected, I begin to relax. More impossible wonder! This place could not possibly be in the golden space craft, for it seems that the dunes parade endlessly into the distance. Unsure of what to do, I walk over toward what looks like a six-foot-tall grass tree. In my physical reality, they are one of my favorite plants, so this is something familiar. As I walk, I notice a very fine, hairlike plant growing over the sand, so fine it is hardly visible. The fact that it is a pale blue color no longer seems odd. The grass tree is reassuring, even though its long sweeping needle-thin, grasslike foliage is a deep blue.

Standing by the tree, I stroke the foliage in the way I often physically do, when an odd thing happens. Tiny sparks of light—not electrical—leap from the foliage to my hands, and they carry a communication. As each spark of light touches me, it ignites an inner knowing.

Amazed, I realize that this grass tree look-alike is an intelligent, aware entity. Although in Australia we have a physical tree that looks rather similar (Xanthorrhoea), it is not the same. This entity does not have a three-dimensional counterpart. The environment in which we are meeting duplicates its home world, but as far as I know, we are still on the golden craft.

As I follow my compulsion to stroke the grass tree Being, a particularly large spark of light ignites a vast insight. This insight is in the form of vision, inner knowing, and pure experience all rolled up into one package. It takes me less than a micromoment to receive it, but some timeless moments to assimilate it. In essence, the grass tree Being reveals that on Earth there are spiritual Beings of pure energy in every plant, from our tiny lichens to the huge trees. Although the death of a plant does not disrupt or disturb the spiritual Beings that express their energy in the plants, it does cause a displacement. In those moments of displacement—measured in hours, months, or even years on Earth—the Beings of energy that express through the forms of plant life, return instantly to their metaphysical realm of pure spirit. Would I like to visit this realm?

The other insight that bowls me over is that I know this entity. In some other nonphysical realm, I have shared experience with this Being that appears like a blue grass tree. It does not reveal any more about our relationship than this, and I realize that it is probably wisest not to; what I do not know or remember cannot upset me emotionally.

The grass tree Being is aware of my acceptance of the offer before I even attempt to confirm it, and I ponder on how we will get to this other realm of plant spirit.

The foliage rustles gently, encouraging me once again to caress the needle-fine fronds. As I do so, a huge burst of sparkling lights dazzles me, engulfing me in a brilliant shower of illumination. And I am elsewhere.

I gaze around me in awe. I am surrounded by a non-physical realm of stunning beauty. For a while I just stand awe-stricken, trying to adjust to a reality where nothing seems to follow any physical law, or to conform to any normality of Earth.

I stand in the midst of what I can only describe as dozens of ethereal waterfalls, varying in size from a tiny wisp to immeasurably large torrents, all surrounded by a profusion of plants and flowers. But none of this is physical. The waterfalls are of liquid light, rather like the lagoon of liquid light, but where that was calm and tranquil, this is an explosion of dynamic energy. Tiny fragments of rainbow hang in a shimmering haze around the waterfalls, consciously exploring all the colors of our known spectrum and beyond. Oddly, every waterfall that I can see appears to be a different color. Instead of being a clear and colorless fluid, the water has the clarity of wine with a bewildering range of color. Cardinal and pale rose reds flow side by side with champagne pinks, chartreuse and apricot yellows, saffron golds, cerulean and ice blues, emerald greens, and every other tone and hue of color possible.

I am dumbfounded by an energy that is so overwhelmingly powerful in this incomprehensible world that our own physical Nature is a pale echo by comparison. And yet, this *is* Nature; it is the nonphysical Spirit of Nature in a very different realm of expression. This is a matrix where plant life is conceived in consciousness, before its eventual birth into the infinite and varied realms of reality— including our physical Earth reality.

Nothing here conforms to human expectation. The streams follow a vibrant earth in some places, to lift into the air, supported by nothing as they span a gulf or simply change direction. Some waterfalls are falling water, while others are water flowing upward! There seems to be no birds or animals, but large butterfly-like insects flit around in profusion. As I gaze at one beautiful specimen near me, its wings open and close gently. Startled, I gasp in surprise. It has no body. The wings simply join at the base, so that it is no more than flying wings. As I study it, I notice that this particular butterfly has mirror-surfaced wings, each reflecting the myriad of color around it as it flies. How a bodiless pair of wings can exist is beyond me, but then, this whole reality is beyond my comprehension.

Not sure of how to move around in a reality as odd as this, I take a hesitant step and gasp in delight. While I am not exactly flying, I am floating as I walk. It feels unbelievably free! Walking over to a pink waterfall, I plunge my light-body hand into it, and a surge of healing peace flows through me. Wonderful! Floating over to a flame-red stream, I again put my hand in. This time I feel a surge of active energy. Feeling very daring, I float/walk over to a ten-foot waterfall of the exact shade of violet as the violets I used to pick in my aunt's orchard as a child, and I step into it. An incredible surge of clarity, peace, and upliftment flows through me. It feels that the water is inside me rather than flowing over my body, and I realize with astonishment that it is. In some way, the ethereal liquid flows right through my Being.

This immersion must be making my senses more acute, opening my cognition, for I suddenly become aware of other Beings—and the Song. Once again, the Song is pervading All That Is, echoing from every waterfall in a uniquely different tone as it registers the different shades of color. It occurs to me that the Song is the creative factor here, that everything I can see, and all that is beyond my perception, is an expression of the Song. I somehow know that the butterfly creatures are also the Song in movement, an expression of joy in flight.

The Beings that I see are both familiar and startlingly new. I recognize them as spirits of Nature, but never have I seen such diversity as now. Many of these Nature Beings radiate a Light around them that takes on the flickering shape of the plant form through which they express on a physical Earth. Oddly, size is not a factor in this. I see a Nature Being that seems to reflect oak trees in its radiance, yet the Being is no larger than another Nature Being that reflects yellow primroses. Both of these Nature Beings are quite large, reflecting an aura of Light that is about thirty to fifty feet high and perhaps half as far across. I perceive the Nature Beings within the radiating Light as the source of the illumination. In the way that a human body is flesh in appearance, these Beings appear as solid Light. Their bodies seem to be far more solid than my light body is. Unlike a human, they have no discernible shape, for their bodies of solid Light flicker and change in the manner of a flame. However, beyond all this, I am aware of great focus and intelligence. There is not a trace of identity in them, or any personality as we know it, yet their focus is so *absolute* that for me it serves to easily identify them.

Since stepping under the violet waterfall, my insight, like an unfolding bud, has been steadily expanding. I perceive that although these Nature Beings are intelligent, they are not intellectual. Their intelligence is of a purity and focus beyond human comprehension. They are reservoirs of a vast *knowing,* yet this knowing cannot be transmitted in any way other than by direct experience. They can, if they wish, ignite a knowing within us. This is then verbalized through our intellects and invariably distorted in direct accordance to our beliefs and conditioning.

As I float/walk among these Nature Beings — and there

are great numbers of them—I see other Nature Beings who appear very different. There are a few Beings who do not contain the energy of plants within their radiance. Some seem to hold the substance of stone around them, not in form, but in a subtle vibrating essence. Others hold the feeling of a great boulder, some a precious mineral, and some seem as though they belong deep within our physical Earth. Each is a Nature Being of solid Light, but they reflect as a far more dense physicality than the Beings of a plant expression.

I thought that I was reasonably familiar with the diminutive elfin Nature spirits, but the profusion of tiny, glowing spirits of Nature in this realm is prodigious. In the manner of a cloud of flickering fireflies on a warm summer evening, these minute Beings swarm in every space and over every plant of this fabulous kingdom. And they are of varieties beyond description. Some appear as pure sparks of light, while others are as if shards of rainbow; some are opaque, some appear solid, some like bits of jellyfish, and some like sparks of incandescent fire. One type I have never encountered before appears as sparks of opalescent jet-black. The overall appearance is one of mobile, intelligent sparkling Beings of Light. All these tiny Nature spirits seem to stay within close proximity to one another, never straying far apart. This creates the effect of clouds of sparkling ethereal illumination. There are others, however, that are not so small. Many of the Nature spirits are about half my height and powerfully illumined. Within the light of their illumination, I see the suggestion of faun, elf, fairy, gnome, leprechaun, sprite, and others, all in the

160

classic way of our stories and conditioning. As I gaze at them, spellbound, I cannot help but wonder if they hold the nebulous identity of a form taken from human minds, or if, indeed, the reverse is true.

I float/walk for a long way, the waterways gradually becoming less, while the vegetation goes through a subtle change. Near the water, it was lush and abundant, with large plants carrying leaves of every color imaginable, and I found it disconcerting to see leaves of a transparent pink, or deep ink blue. Now, however, the vegetation is more like true grass trees, with bright green foliage. This time, I feel sure that they are plants. I stop near one to stroke the foliage, but there are no sparks of light, no inner communication.

As I continue wandering aimlessly on my way, I notice that the light is becoming greener. Green light is not like our daylight; it is strange, to put it mildly. Abruptly, I get the distinct impression that I am being guided and that I am exactly where I should be. Turning toward a small hill, covered in delicate, pale green, cuplike plants, which, as with all the other vegetation, are covered in tiny Nature spirits, I float/walk to the top. I'm glad that I am floating, for the beautiful cup plants are tissue thin, and I do not want to inadvertently crush them. I get the impression that the plants are so delicate that even my light body would be too heavy for their fragility. The hill is taller than I thought, and I go higher and higher, floating without effort over the plants.

How very strange! I am now ten times higher than the hill originally appeared, and I am not yet at the top. Most odd! The hill is not steep, and continues to look small, but I am maybe a thousand feet above the area of waterfalls. On and on I go, climbing in an effortless float up and up the small hill. I have no idea of time, and, obviously, distance is equally meaningless. I estimate that I could now be as high as five thousand feet above the multicolored waterfalls. As I float/walk ever higher up this deceptive hillside, the light is steadily getting greener. It is as clear around me as normal bright daylight, except that it is now a powerful and brilliant green.

Without warning, I reach the top of the hill, and I gasp in sheer astonishment. Before me, standing with its base in a deep, deep valley and towering into the air far above me, so high the top disappears from my view, is an incredible glasslike Pillar. Stunned, I just stand and gape. It is beautiful, bizarre, and utterly awe-inspiring. The Pillar is a glowing, incandescent, pulsating emerald green. It is brilliant beyond luminosity, and it is Aware! I stare unmoving, held by this resplendent sight.

I have no idea how long I stand, mesmerized. Tears trickle from my eyes, and I am aware that my physical self in bed is also affected. It is not only what I am seeing, but also what I am feeling; the Green Light touches my soul. All that I am is totally involved. Standing before this mystic Pillar is a deeply transcendental experience; it is somehow absolute.

I become aware that the Pillar is the source of this realm. It is the creative factor of this reality, its reason for being. The Green Light now dominates everything with its incandescent emerald clarity; it radiates from the Pillar and carries an energy that has no human terms of translation. I could say that it is the energy source of all life within this realm, but it goes far beyond this. The radiant Green Light is a total nourishment for all the Beings of Nature — the myriad spirits of Nature that inhabit our planet Earth. As I feel the Green Light permeating me, my insight continues to expand. Our Earth would not be able to express a physical Nature without this metaphysical realm and its Pillar of Green Light. From the greatest to the most tiny, all the Nature Beings of Earth constantly flicker in and out of frames of reality from Earth to this realm and back, each movement beyond time, but vital for the continuity of life as we know it.

The Pillar and the Song are One. The Green Light is the Song; the Song manifests as the Green Light. I gaze at the Nature Beings who, in countless numbers, fly bathing in the emerald Green Light. Just as we humans are spiritual Beings of Light who purposefully incarnate into a physical Earth realm, so, too, the Light Beings of Nature are purposefully involved on a physical Earth. We share a purpose, but we do not share an awareness of this. Unseen by human eyes, unloved by us, unknown and unappreciated, even scorned and rejected as "fairy tales," these spirits of Nature are a major factor in all life on Earth. Without their power of creativity, without the Song that expresses Intelligence beyond the DNA, without the mystical Pillar and its energy of Green Light recharging and nourishing the spirits of Nature, our physical Earth would become totally barren.

I walk to the very edge of the hill I have climbed, noting

how it drops sheer away into the deep valley where the base of the incredible Pillar is centered. Well over three hundred feet in diameter and ice smooth, the Pillar seems to grow from the very heart of this metaphysical realm.

Without a thought, I leap out toward the Pillar of Green Light, uncaring of any consequence. At first I begin to fall, but within moments I am drawn to the Pillar as though a metal filing to a vast and powerful magnet. As I float closer and closer to the Pillar and its Green luminosity of Light, I approach ecstasy, soul nourishment, total rapture. I am held in the radiance of the Green Light, experiencing Love as the continual expanding essence of all creation, and everything gradually fades away.

As I become aware again, I am stroking the needlelike foliage of the blue, grass tree Being. I have no idea how I got to that realm of Nature spirits, or back again, but I am too overfilled to even contemplate it.

8

Travelers of the Multiverse

Earth life appears to be finite,
but in a Greater Reality it is infinite.
Despite an infinite potential,
most people focus only on a finite reality.
This denies our greatest opportunities
and our truth of Self,
for we are, essentially, Beings of infinity.

Stunned by my adventure, I stand mute for what seems a long no-time. I stay near the grass tree Being while I allow the overwhelming impact of my experience to settle. Idly, without any attention to what I am doing, my hands caress the needle-fine foliage of the entity, and a small, sparkling shower of light enfolds me. Once again, in its unique way of communicating, I get more insight into all that is happening to me. I learn that the wonderful realm of Nature Beings is yet another frame of reality, and that my focus of self was pulsed into this realm under the influence and guidance of the grass tree Being. Yet, at the same time, I have remained where I now stand! I learn that each one of us is always experiencing many realities simultaneously, but our focus determines which reality we relate to. For most people, their focus on a physical, three-dimensional reality never wavers. This creates an equally unwavering belief that no other realms of reality exist.

166

The grass tree Being gives me no indication of where its home reality/realm is, nor of its name or species. However, it does give me an impression of it and others of its kind swimming upright through the loose, dry sand and hair plant combination of its environment. It appears to move with about the same ease and speed that we walk on the ground. I learn that it has a symbiotic relationship with the prolific hairlike plant, each nourishing the other as the grass tree Being moves around.

The communication of impressions fade, and I realize that it is time for me to move on. Even as this thought crosses my mind, the door through which I entered into the room of the grass tree Being is again visible. How it vanished, only to appear again when needed, is yet another mystery. Bidding a silent "farewell and thank you" to the grass tree Being, I walk over to the door, open it, and step into the long, familiar corridor. As I close the door, I notice the room now appears quite a normal size, with the strange entity flowing smoothly across it, scarcely disturbing the sand as it travels.

Alone, I wander down the corridor, passing several other closed doors. I am at a loss as to where to go, for in either direction there is nothing but the long, wide, seemingly endless corridor, and the doors. I keep hoping that the Shepherd will show up, but the place seems deserted. Not all the doors are the same. Some are very formal, yet colorful, while others appear in various styles, ranging from high and wide to short and narrow. Whether this gives any indication about the entities that dwell within, I have no idea. I walk past quite a number of really strange closed doors, when a reasonably normal, pale gray door framed in metallic silver suddenly swings wide open.

About six feet tall, elegant and lean, a catlike Being is smiling at me from an oddly familiar face. Dense, microshort, golden fur covers its entire body. Its face has a natural, expressive smile, and my immediate touch of apprehension evaporates.

"How wonderful to see you again, Michael," it says, speaking directly into my mind.

"Do I know you from somewhere?" I ask, feeling rather silly, for I have no recollection of such an entity, although he/she/it certainly "feels" familiar. "Perhaps I've met you in some other reality. I feel that I know you, but where or when I don't know." I feel foolish and inadequate.

The creature smiles, its expression of profound sympathy helping me to feel more comfortable.

"Will the truth cause you too much anguish?" it asks, not waiting for my reply. "You and I have spent much time together, even though it was within a timeless reality." The smile becomes more pronounced, and a filament rolls slowly across each of its round, silver, moonlike eyes. "You always referred to me as a he, even though I have no gender. My name is Seine [pronounced C-ine]. Please, do not be embarrassed if you do not remember me. Your heart carries my memory, and I am honored by this. You could not possibly survive your Earth incarnations if you carried *all* your memories mentally intact."

"I feel ashamed. To know you and still not be able to recognize you—that's terrible."

"Not so. Even memories of past physical lives are quite

168

rare in humanity. It can cause great confusion in a race that basically denies its own continuity of Self. But to remember life in other realities and other dimensions without adequate preparation could cause insanity. Only now is this omnipresent memory awakening among your people, and even this is only by those who are making that a conscious choice." He smiles wryly. "And, paradoxically, even those who consciously choose are seldom aware that they have made the choice! What a complicated people you have become."

"Will I forget you again when I leave this reality?"

Seine's silver orb eyes are very expressive, and I read my answer in the regret and sympathy I see in them.

"Yes, Michael, you will. But the probability is very strong that you and I will meet again, and you will remember. This will be when you Awaken and realize Self." He smiles gently. "It is ironic that you will not remember any of this meeting or conversation until you Awaken. Even then, you will not remember until the right timing."

"Is there a reason for this?"

"Your probability pattern suggests that in the immediate future you will strenuously attempt to reject this greater metaphysical Reality. The less trauma you have to deal with after you leave this timeless realm, the better."

"That makes sense, knowing me," I reply glumly. "But why can't I remember this as soon as I Awaken?"

"Timing, Michael. Timing is everything."

His comment about my Awakening suddenly registers. "The Shepherd spoke about when I Awaken, and now you have. I take it this means I *will* Awaken?"

"Is that not the destination of all humanity?"

"You're very evasive, aren't you? Why don't you help me to Awaken by answering my questions with direct answers?"

"I am helping you to Awaken, but I do it in the way that most pertains to your growth, character, and timing. Would a fledgling eagle learn to be a master of the sky if its mother always carried it on her back?"

What can I say to that? "But you *are* saying that it's very probable that I will Awaken in this incarnation?"

"The probability is there, yes."

I grin gleefully. "Okay, I'll settle for that."

Seine looks at me pensively. "Have you been into any of the rooms along this corridor?"

"Yes. The Shepherd took me into a room with sand dunes and a grass tree Being. Who or what is that?"

Seine has a wide smile. "If that entity did not tell you, then it is obviously not appropriate."

"Well, at least tell me if it is a plant or an animal."

"Actually, it is neither. Animal, mineral, and vegetable may well define all life on a three-dimensional Earth, but it is quite inadequate for a Greater Reality."

I look at Seine skeptically. "Really?"

"Tell me, Michael, in your light body, are you animal, mineral, or vegetable?"

My mouth opens, then closes. "Point taken!"

"I take it that the grass tree introduced you to the realm of Nature Beings?" Seine asks mischievously.

"Yes. My God! The Pillar of Green Light!"

Seine nods thoughtfully, his catlike ears twitching. "Yes,

I can imagine the impact for you, although this is not the first time you have stood within its radiance."

I feel sad that such rich memories are unavailable to me. "Has it been in any recent incarnation?"

He shakes his head. "No, it was in a much earlier time frame of your reality. You were a very powerful mystic, even if a mite uncontrollable."

I feel wistful. "I wish I could remember all that. Maybe that's why I leapt toward the Pillar without even a thought of fear or falling."

"Probably, yes," Seine replies, "although it is not possible to experience fear within the radiance of the Pillar. Believe it or not, fear as you know it is a human product, based in your conditioning and imagination."

He glances up the corridor, suddenly brisk.

"Come on, it's time you met some of your fellow travelers. One word of caution: Although some are humanoid in shape, they are not Earth-type human. A few of the entities you will meet are very different, neither humanoid nor vaguely like anything you can physically relate to. However, you know several of them, so perhaps a few more memories might come back to you."

Agitated, I grab his furred arm. "Er, do I have to do anything?"

Seine gives me a puzzled look. "Such as?"

"I don't know," I reply in exasperation. "It's just that I'm not used to this. I have met some strange entities already in this metaphysical state, but those encounters just happened."

"Michael, just be yourself," he says, amused.

Somewhat reassured, I walk beside him along the wide corridor. "How is it possible for such a long corridor to be in such a small craft? How can it possibly contain all this, and the rooms? It doesn't make sense."

"Not physically, no. This craft follows the continuum principle. Within this craft, all space is available in an infinite continuum." Seine shrugs expressively. "How do I explain a principle that has no meaning in your terms? In here, space follows a different rule; thus it appears that this corridor is endless. In actuality it is not, but in the reality we have created, it is. A continuum is where a finite state, or space, becomes infinite. Both realities are true, but you cannot discern between them. In a similar way, Earth life appears to be finite, but in a Greater Reality it is infinite. Despite an infinite potential, most people focus only on a finite reality, thus limiting both opportunities and potential. You, Michael, are developing the focus of an infinite Reality. Does that explain it?"

Oddly enough, I understand. "If we focus on our immortality instead of our mortality, and on continuity instead of beginnings and endings, will that change our reality and our experience of life?"

"Of course it will. You are doing just that. A greater focus expands your awareness. With an expanded awareness, you perceive more and experience more of the *Greater* Reality. And so it continues. That's only natural."

"It seems pretty simple."

"It is. Simple is also powerful."

As we talk, we are walking past quite a number of doors.

"These doors seem to go on and on forever. Whatever is behind them?" I ask.

"Generally speaking, they are the home environments of the travelers on this craft. The same continuum principle applies to each of them. In each average-size room is the potential for an extended Reality. So the rooms are a finite size that fits within this craft, while a simultaneous infinity also holds true. A very convenient arrangement all around. It means that a small craft has the potential of a large planet."

I am stunned by the immense potential of such a Reality.

"The ultimate answer to overcrowding in our larger cities!" I gasp.

"That could well be, but only after you have learned the lessons that precede it," Seine murmurs.

We walk briskly past a few more doors, the corridor stretching endlessly before us, when Seine comes to a stop.

"This is the meeting room of the travelers and craft personnel," he says, indicating we will enter it.

The door is the biggest I have seen, nearly twenty feet tall and about as wide. "Are there some big guys in there or what?" I ask apprehensively.

Seine chuckles, his mouth showing multiple rows of pale blue vestigial teeth. "Very big, Michael, very big."

The door vanishes as he faces it. It does not open or slide or roll up—it disappears, and I am completely unprepared for what I see. I stare into a room filled with such a bizarre assortment of entities that had I been alone I would have fled. I clutch Seine's arm weakly.

"My God!"

Chuckling, Seine asks, "Has it ever occurred to you that you are a strange entity to many others?"

The room I am staring into is about twice the size of a football field. Oddly, I can see it all in the same perspective. What is distant appears visually as close and clear as the immediate area. It is furnished—if that is the right description—with a bewildering assortment of chairs, stools, perches, cushions, floating pads, and a wide range of unidentifiable paraphernalia.

But the occupants! My grip on Seine's arm tightens. "Don't leave me. Please don't leave me here." I gasp, trembling, as I look around. There are some slender, delicate appearing, five-foot tall humanoids with translucent blue skin, who seem so familiar and known, yet so unutterably far removed from my reality that I am almost overwhelmed.

Seine takes my chin gently in one hand and turns my head toward him. His eyes meet mine, holding my gaze, and very clear and soft in the silence of our communication, I hear his words, "It's all right, Michael. Everything is under control."

I get the distinct impression that it is I who am under control, for on hearing his words I am immediately calm and accepting.

Seine must be reading my mind. "You are not under my control," he adds. "I have simply put aside your conditioned fears and reaction. You do not need them."

How right he is. Without fear, I obviously do not feel threatened. I feel curious, ready to meet these other Beings and learn from them. Without my fear, I get an insight into the terrible restrictions and confinement fear places us in, denying us our abilities and potential.

Overall, the room is lighted with a mellow, white illumination, but in certain areas a very different color either lights it or changes the whole spectrum of vision. I get the impression that some areas are infrared, while others are beyond my understanding. Although in these special areas of illumination there is no obvious demarcation, the different light does not seep into other areas. One area is pitch-dark, yet, strangely, I can perceive vague forms moving within it. Without a doubt, Reality on this craft is limitless.

Seine and I have only taken a few paces into the room, when I am confronted by a smiling humanlike Being.

"Welcome, my friend."

Humanlike could be misleading! This very masculine entity is not much over three feet tall, but he has the stature of a very big, super-heavy, human weight lifter, compressed and compacted. Not dwarfish, because he is not malformed, he has a thickness and immensity of limb that is prodigious. He is truly a midget giant!

"Er, thank you. Do I know you?" I ask.

His head is nearly as wide as my shoulders, and he has a veritable thicket of black hair on his head and eyebrows. His face is without hair, while his craggy features are more deeply seamed than I would have thought possible. He carries an aura of unassailable strength, mixed with a friendly humor. Wearing a belted, one piece tunic of some dark green material, his mischievous, ice-gray eyes are laughing at me.

"You not remember me?" he asks in mock concern. His incredibly deep voice seems to echo up from the vast cavern of his chest.

I shrug. "Er, no. I'm sorry."

With a bellowing laugh, he hugs me. Startled, I learn that my light body has some density in the environment of this craft, for it feels how I would expect to feel if hugged by a short but massive gorilla under normal physical conditions. Gasping at his crushing strength, ineffectually but spontaneously, I attempt to hug him.

"I am Skarl," he says in the subterranean voice that I hear both audibly and telepathically.

I am consumed by curiousity. "You seem to break all the rules," I gasp breathlessly. "The Shepherd and Seine have nonphysical bodies, and I am in my light body, but you seem to be physical. How is this possible?"

"Means you not know all rules," he replies with a laugh. "Come, I show you how."

Beckoning, he marches away with short, heavy, clumping footsteps, and I look inquiringly at Seine.

"Go with him, Michael. You are quite safe, and you *are* old friends. I will be here when you return."

Reassured, I rush after Skarl. As I hurry to catch up, I notice something very odd. When I looked into this room from the doorway, I could see pretty much the whole room, but now that I am in it, I cannot see any of the other entities, or the weird paraphernalia. The room appears to be just an average size, with only Skarl and me in it. Skarl stops so suddenly I run into him, with all the impact of hitting an average brick wall.

"Why you in hurry?" he asks.

"I'm not in a hurry," I protest. "I'm trying to keep up with you. Where has everyone gone? Where's the big room? And how is it that you are so solid?"

Skarl's grin stretches from ear to ear across a wide expanse of deeply seamed face. "I joke! I find it funny you not remember me! Funny you not know how this all works."

Abruptly, I am hit by a startling idea. "What was my name when you knew me?"

"Mekon, of course. Why?"

"Mekon," I say, savouring the word. It strikes a chord deep within, stirring and igniting long dormant memories, and I know that he speaks the truth. "Mekon. How strange that I should not even know my true name. Mekon must be my universal name. I am presently known as Michael."

"Michael, hmmm. I like."

"Seine was telling me about the continuum principle, and how finite and infinite realities share the same space. Is that how all this works?" I ask, waving my arms around me to indicate the room and us.

"Yes, same principle with refinements." Skarl thumped one enormous fist on the broad expanse of his chest. "By using refinements, I am physically here in finite reality, and metaphysically here in infinite Reality at same moment. My focus determines reality. Watch, I change it."

For a moment Skarl's outline seems to blur, then he becomes clear. He appears the same in detail, but his energy as a Being is quite subtly altered. I can now sense and perceive his Lightness of Being. He smiles at me, the same wide, craggy smile. "Take my hand," he invites, his hand extended toward me.

When our hands touch, the difference is very apparent. He is no longer physical. The fingers of his light hand curl around mine in a tight grasp, and he touches the belt around his tunic. "Relax; you safe with Skarl."

For what seem long moments, I get the impression of racing headlong down a long, long tunnel at tremendous speed, then all is calm. Skarl lets go of my hand. "This is my home." He indicates all around him.

My first, overwhelming sensation is of crushing weight, yet it is not physical. I stretch, somehow trying to resist a pressure, when all at once, I understand. This is a planet of heavy gravity. Whereas Earth has 14.7 pounds per square inch of atmospheric pressure, this place must far exceed it.

"Three times Earth gravity." Skarl answers my unspoken question.

I glance around me at a planet of contradictions. I would have thought that a planet with a heavy, dense gravity would be reasonably flat and compressed, but nothing could be further from the truth. Growing from solid rock are large forests of a strange formation of growth that looks remarkably like gigantic coral, rearing maybe three hundred to six hundred feet into the air.

I gasp, indicating the thin, coral-like growth. "That's incredible. What is it?"

"You have trees; we have larsig."

"Er, is larsig a plant, like a tree?"

"I just say that," Skarl replies.

They do not look at all like trees. Although they have no leaves, there are clusters of thin, knobbly, budlike objects all over each towering larsig. The rock they are growing from is glass-smooth and flat as a tennis court, adding to the overall bizarre contrast.

I look at Skarl. "This is weird. Heavy gravity, smooth flat rock, yet towering coral-like plants."

Skarl shakes his head emphatically. "Not weird—home." He then touches his belt again, somewhere on the large buckle, and with a slight shimmering of his body, he is again powerfully physical. He beckons to me. "Come."

"Is your atmosphere anything like ours?" I ask him. "Is it breathable for humans?"

"Similarities, " he says, never one to waste words. "We need nitrogen; you need oxygen. This atmosphere very compressed, very cold. Physically, you die instantly here." He suddenly spins around, hands outstretched in a theatrical gesture. "For me, beautiful, stagmarg. For you, deadly."

"Stagmarg? What's that?"

He stares at me thoughtfully, then gestures to the sky. "Stagmarg, stagmarg, up there."

"Ah, I get it. You mean heavenly."

Having stared skyward, I notice that the sky is the same color as Skarl's eyes—ice gray, yet there appears to be three white suns that are obviously much closer than our own sun. I have never even considered cool suns before. Even in my light body, I am aware that this is a cold, frigid place.

"We only have one sun," I tell him, "and it's hot."

He nods. "I know Earth planet. I am a traveler of the multiverse."

"What's a multiverse?"

Skarl takes a deep breath. "You ask lot of questions about things you already know. Multiverse is the Greater Reality of universe. Humans physically experience universe in linear time. Metaphysically, same universe is multiverse in spherical time—all in present moment."

I get it. When physical, I relate to a physical reality, which is universal, but in my light body I am experiencing the same universe as a timeless multiverse of endless possibilities.

We walk only a short distance on the glass-smooth rock before we reach a large door embedded into the rock. It reminds me of a big manhole cover, except that it is perfectly square. Skarl grabs the door, lifting it open as though a featherweight. As I listen to the solid thud of it hitting the rock, I get the impression of great weight.

"Do you understand our weight system?" I ask him.

Skarl nods vigorously.

"How much do you weigh in your physical body?"

He calculates briefly. "Over half a ton."

"My God," I gasp involuntarily. "I knew you were dense and solid, but I didn't realize it was to that degree."

He grins that great, wide smile. "We proper physical. Humans are powder puffs." Laughing uproariously, he wipes his watering eyes. "Old joke between us," he explains.

I follow him down a flight of broad, wide stairs, brightly lit by some hidden source. The ceiling is well above my head, which I find odd, considering the people here are so short. We go only a little way before reaching a large room. I look around for the source of the light but cannot locate it. It seems that all the walls glow.

"How do you get this light?" I ask Skarl.

"Mix chemical, spray on rock wall. It react, making light for long time," he replies.

Some chemical! Not only are the walls illuminated, but they also have the appearance of smooth, pinkish glass. A very beautiful effect.

As I walk further into the room, I realize that this is a very high-tech place. For some reason, I had not expected this, yet it should have been apparent that Skarl is familiar with both a physical and a metaphysical technology far beyond human terms. The room has about a dozen very sturdy one- and two-person consoles, built of what appears as smooth, pale pink plastic or glass. Each unit is very low to the ground, and each is occupied. A low dome of some transparent material covers each unit, sealing it.

"Is it any good my asking the name of this planet and who you people are?" I ask Skarl.

His expression is wry. "This planet Larsaas Zi; we are Oans. Larsaas Zi is within what you call Milky Way, part of your own galaxy. Near, yet far away."

I have the feeling it is far more than distance that separates our planets and people. As I watch the Oans within the domed consoles, one of them abruptly disappears.

"Where has he gone?"

"Female! She has entered reality of six dimension. Three-dimension physical body displaced to accommodate this."

"So what happens to her body?"

"In another reality frame. Same place, different frame."

"This makes human reality feel prehistoric!"

"Not so. Humans learn different lessons — different purpose in being. Humans very admirable; tough lessons."

"Tell me, Skarl, why am I here with you? Why not a scientist? All this is wasted on the likes of me. I mean, if

I could only understand how to recreate your light source, I would make a personal fortune and give something of value to humanity. But it's all beyond me."

"Such things are not your purpose. You develop self to make this possible for a very long time. You much more than you think you are. This not physical science; this is technology of Reality and Being. You share your experiences with other people one day. It is important, for many will recognize and know." He indicates his people in the consoles. "We work toward a common purpose, an Awakening of Intelligent Beings in several frames of reality. Physical Earth one such frame."

"Where do I fit into all this?"

"In proper timing, write and share self."

"If I do, most people will think I'm mad."

"Not matter. The few will not. The few as important as the many—more important in times of change."

"How will I know the right timing?"

Skarl's arms fling dramatically to the ceiling. "Your questions, do they never stop? You will know. Accept."

Together, we walk among the consoles, but all I see is a flickering range of lights and dials that are completely incomprehensible to me. Skarl describes several more available functions that they can do, mostly involving travel between realities. I learn that it is the consoles that allow him to move so easily between Larsaas Zi and the craft. His belt buckle is a remote control to their technology.

For a while Skarl leaves me while he enters another room. When he returns, he beckons. "Come, we return."

He touches his buckle, once again shimmering into his

light body. Taking my hand, he touches the buckle again. Once more there is a sensation of traveling at speed down a very long tunnel. Then we are in the craft. "Next time, you remember," Skarl says, with his wide grin. "You go now, meet others." Then he hugs me. This time he is still in his light body, and the hug is very different. The power and strength are more a suggestion than a reality, while the hug is like a fusion of our Beingness.

I wander away, realizing as I leave him how much Skarl has shown me about other, very different, three-dimensional humanoids. For some reason, my feet seem to want to walk toward a very brightly illuminated area, so I follow my impulse. As I walk, I pass the zone of several other very strange entities.

In one zone of dim yellow light, I see a couple of pale creatures that look remarkably like large pythons, only they each have a multitude of thin legs in the manner of a millipede. I feel them in my mind, whispering in a soft caress. "Come in, Mekon. We are your friends."

That clinches it! If they know me as Mekon, then they probably know more about me than I do. I walk into their zone. Close up, they are big. They have the abundant legs for about half their body length. They flow along the ground, fast and very smooth. The upper half of the body has a few long, thick ropelike tentacles that seem to hug the body, only unfurling when needed for manipulating objects. This they do with uncanny dexterity. The body is about my waist thick, with the upper half reaching nearly ten feet high. The head destroys the snake appearance completely and is a shock. Although it is in direct proportion to the body, it is shaped rather like a large dustbin lid, or Frisbee, sitting flat on the top of the long body. It appears to have no eyes, mouth, nose, ears, or other human features, but there is a constantly moving frill of tiny tendrils around the entire outer perimeter of its head. I get the impression that it is incalculably efficient in its extrasensory capacity.

Now that I am close to them, I notice the beautiful and delicate network of dark, lacelike amber that webs their pale bodies. The overall impression is devastatingly alien.

Rather rudely, I stare at them in utter astonishment.

"Obviously, you do not remember us."

It is not a question, and I can only shake my head, as I continue to stare in wonder. "I had no idea that anything like you exists."

"We are amused."

Even as they tell me, I can feel their amusement. Suddenly, as though jolted from me, I gasp at a surge of powerful, clear, and very old memories.

"Wait! I do remember. You are the entire personnel on this craft. You and the Shepherd. You two act in unison, as if one Being. You share one mind, yet you each have your own. You are each an aspect of the other. This is a unique characteristic of your race, yet it is extremely rare. When this happens your abilities quadruple. I remember! You come from a planet that is sixth or seventh dimension, with an unpronounceable name.

"I also remember that this is your true form, but you spend far more time as light bodies. You breathe and are nourished by inhaling pure light. I remember that although you look so big and heavy, you weigh very little by my standard."

I am excited that I remember so much. "Did you jog my memory, or did it just happen?"

"We ignite your consciousness, but it is you who create the recall. You will forget again when you leave this craft and your light-body focus, but in timing with the expansion of your awareness and soul growth, you will once again remember. This whole experience is designed to open you to All That Is. Life is *not* all three-dimensional and human. Before you return to the stars you have to encompass a Greater Reality."

I inner-feel their focus turning to other things, and they confirm it.

"We thank you for your courage and capacity. We await the moment we travel together again."

Leaving their zone of filtered yellow light, I continue on my way toward the brightly illuminated area. What attracts me I do not know, but I am drawn as though by a magnet. Astonishingly, the very bright illumination is also confined to its own zone, so I do not realize how powerful it is until I enter the light. With physical eyes I would be blinded, but within this illumination I perceive rather than see, even though vision is perfectly clear.

I seem to be surrounded by dancing flames of light, each flame a brilliant white and moving freely around. Although not really constant, they are approximately the size of a human body, appearing rather as a stretched out drop of water, with the wide end uppermost. A few of them hover around me, and I feel a touch of inquiry that I cannot translate. One flame entity comes closer, slowly and gently, then, as though knowing I will permit it, engulfs me.

Instantly, everything changes. The consciousness of the flame entity merges with mine. I am on a sun, surrounded by coruscating light. I am aware that by three-dimensional terms I am in an inferno of fiery heat, and that no physical life could possibly exist, but in the terms of a Greater Reality, there is no heat at all.

I consciously merge with an Intelligence so awesome in its awareness of life that I, as a human, am no more than a cell in its body of illumination. This Being is pure spirit, expressing Oneness. Each flamelike entity is consciously and knowingly a cell of the One Intelligence. And as a part of the One, it is also the One in a part. Abruptly, I *know* why I am here. Exactly as I perceive and experience the Oneness of this Flame Being, so, too, this is our human truth. The individual *is* the Whole—All That Is—and the Whole *is* the individual. In the Reality of this sun and the entities of flame, separation has no meaning. It does not exist. Our human truth of Oneness/individuality is no less than on this sun, yet our focus and awareness are based in separation.

With this realization so powerfully implanted in my consciousness, I am back in the illumined zone. I feel saddened to realize that there is nothing I can do about this "knowing" until it becomes my experience as a human Being—until I Awaken to the Oneness of All That Is. Even then, I will only be able to share it with others in my natural expression of Love. I have learned already that it is Love that crosses the borders and boundaries of separation, revealing the Principle of Truth.

The flame entities have withdrawn, their purpose fulfilled, and I walk back toward the door. Seine is waiting for me, approval in his moon eyes.

"Come with me; the Shepherd is waiting for you. Your ability to remain in this timeless realm is decreasing, for it draws energy from you in a way that you are unused to, and there is something else you must see and experience. Incidentally, I have a fairly keen sense of what you have been through, and I am delighted with your recall and the way you have assimilated the experience."

I am pleased by his praise. "Thank you. But to tell the truth, I'm still stunned by the diversity of form and Beings here. This is science fiction gone mad. I understand that I may have to share this, one day, but how can I expect acceptance if I tell it as it is? In my world this is loony-bin material.

"Just share it. Life will take care of the details. People will make choices. Some will accept; some will reject. This is not your concern. Just follow your purpose. If you sow the seeds of a Greater Reality, life will determine when and how they grow. Be thankful that your own choice is made."

We are now walking briskly along the corridor again, but within moments Seine stops, and opens a very normal type of door. "Go on in. I will leave you here." When we hug, it is like touching a surge of power as his consciousness enfolds me in Unconditional Love.

"We *will* meet again, Michael. Until then . . ." With a bow of respect, he walks swiftly away.

187

9

A Future
of Your Choice

If you are open to a greater expression of life,
you will expand your reality.
As your reality expands,
you will eventually cross
the intangible metaphysical threshold
into a truly timeless Reality.

For a few moments I hesitate, then I enter. The room seems to be large, having a number of what appear as glass panels along one side. It also seems to be deserted. "Is anyone here?" I call out. Receiving no reply, I walk farther in, crossing over to one of the glass panels. I deliberately leave the door open, so that I do not seem to be surreptitiously snooping around. It occurs to me that the glass panels may be windows, giving me a view of space or whatever it is we are traveling through.

Walking over to the first panel, I discover that they are not windows or, if they are, they are not to the outside of the craft. Each glass panel is about ten feet square and quite clear, but after quickly glancing through a few of them, I realize that each offers a very different view. There are dozens of glass panels all along one very long wall—a wall that now seems to go on and on. These bi-spatial rooms take a bit of getting used to!

Back at the first glass panel, I gaze carefully into the

holographic view that it reveals. I get the impression that it is Earth I am looking at. I have a bird's-eye view, looking down onto an ever-changing scene of an Earth that is unfamiliar to me. I see a city of golden-colored domes, glowing as they absorb the rays of the sun. A faint violet haze is drifting, foglike, across the city. As I watch, the city seems to be coming closer, the domes more detailed. Some of them are quite transparent; many are translucent. I watch as one dome changes from translucent to a golden color, and I wonder if this can be controlled. My bird's-eye view moves closer. People are walking on streets that have no traffic, and no one seems to be in a rush. Trees are prolific, many in full flower. Many of the trees are unknown to me, especially the species with silver colored leaves. The people wear scant but extremely colorful clothing. I am so absorbed in looking at the city that I am startled when a quiet voice interrupts me.

"Do you like what you see?"

Turning around, I see the Shepherd watching me, his blue eyes a reflection of space.

"It's beautiful. Is it Earth?"

"Yes. In all her potential glory."

"I assume that this is Earth's future."

Staring into the window, the Shepherd replies. "Not really. The scene you gaze upon is neither past nor future; it is this moment."

I stare at the Shepherd in confusion. "It can't be. I used to, er . . . I live on Earth, and it's nothing like this."

The Shepherd's eyes are solemn as he turns to me. "If you are going to express a Greater Truth, you must realize that time is not quite as it appears. The past and future are different frames in the Greater Reality of Now—this moment."

With a sudden vivid recollection, the strange scenes I had been compelled to witness in the opaque sphere over the river come back to me. "Does that apply to what I saw within the sphere?" I ask, assuming that the Shepherd will know what I mean. "Was that the past of humanity in a Greater Reality of Now?"

"What you witnessed within the etheric Beings, and within the etheric/physical Beings, was the movement of an evolving Nature into human consciousness. No animal can directly become human, however evolved it may be. Animal consciousness requires a vast expansion to take on the expressions that it will need to assimilate as a human. Learning the laws of free will and imagination as the tools of creation is no minor undertaking."

"Are you saying that when a pet dog or cat is finished in animal evolution, it moves through that etheric development before becoming physically human?"

"That about sums it up."

I stare at the Shepherd, openmouthed. I had never even considered the implications of what happens next to a highly evolved cat or dog or other animal.

"Does this mean they have to go through all those other stages? Even the giants?"

"Not at all. What you saw equates with your present humanity. That is your past, yet it is also a continuity in a different frame of Now. Animal consciousness of today carries a greater awareness. This means that after the earlier etheric and etheric/physical stages, the humanity that develops is self determining. No expression is preordained; this would defeat free will."

My mind is just about overloaded as I try to understand, but one question persists.

"Are those giants doomed forever, or can that be changed? The thought of their terrible violence and suffering going on indefinitely is hard to even think about."

The Shepherd seems pleased with the question. "As you change in the moment, growing in consciousness both individually and as a people, so you alter the future and the past. All time occupies the same space. However, within this timelessness, there are infinite frames of reality. No frame is free from the effect of the eternal Now. Your Now can affect and change their Now."

"This is all too much!"

Gazing back into the holographic view in the glass panel before me, I stare again at the futuristic scene. Time is totally weird. Past and future seem to have no real meaning. I am baffled. The more the Shepherd tells me, the more it seems to open up and the more I need to know. Where does it all end? I shrug. I guess it doesn't!

"So where does this scene fit in?" I ask. "It doesn't belong to the Earth reality that I know."

"Would you like to have it belong?"

"How do I do that?"

"Michael, look at the scene before you. Do you feel a harmonic resonance toward it? Does it fit you?"

"Of course it does," I exclaim. "Wouldn't it fit everyone?"

The Shepherd looks at me with unruffled patience. "No,

Michael, it would not fit everyone. There are many who would want to rip the soil open to exploit its mineral wealth, and others who could not rest until the trees were felled. Yet others would need, in some way, to impose their hand on the imprint of Nature, convinced that they could do it better. There are very few humans who ask Nature if they may co-create together. And what you see now is just such a co-creation. It *is* real. It *does* exist."

"Are you saying I can choose this as my future?" I ask.

"If you belong, yes. You can choose this reality of Earth, or you can choose something quite different. Come, have a look through this next frame."

Following the Shepherd to the next window, I muse over what he has told me. It seems that each window offers a different view of reality, but I am grappling with the mind-boggling implications.

"So are these all different futures for our present humanity, or is only one of them our future?"

The Shepherd raises his eyebrows, looking pensive. "Let me try a different angle to this, Michael. In direct accordance to his or her beliefs and conditioning, there will be a different reality/future for each and every human Being. And each person will believe that his or her experience is the only basic reality there is. This will create the usual dichotomy of a consensus reality which is made of a shared sameness, even though the people concerned each experience only their own reality."

"But . . . but that doesn't make sense!"

"Of course it doesn't. Are you suggesting that human behavior normally does make sense?"

What can I say to that?

"Naturally," the Shepherd continues, "there will always be those people who learn to become more open, eventually experiencing a Greater Reality within this frame. Generally, they are ridiculed and criticized, for this is the way of consensus reality. Paradoxically, however, even consensus reality has many different future frames of Now."

Standing at the next window, the Shepherd gestures toward its view. "This is another future reality."

I look into another frame of Earth reality. Gone is the beauty, gone the peace. The view moves swiftly over a ravaged countryside, green and prolific but strangely and terribly distorted. A city comes into view, contrasting great wealth with shocking poverty. "Is this a consensus reality future?" I whisper.

The Shepherd ignores my question, and holding out a hand invites me to accompany him. "Come and see for yourself, for this is one direction humanity is taking."

I shudder. "No, thank you. I experienced myself in lifetimes of battle earlier, and it was terrible. I don't want to suffer any more trauma like that."

"You will accompany me this time, rather than I accompanying an uncomprehending you. You will be a nonphysical observer, not an active participant."

"You mean I won't get hurt?"

"Guaranteed—no hurt or pain," the Shepherd replies.

"Do you mean to say that you watched all my ordeals as I journeyed, and I didn't know?" I gasp.

"You were never alone, Michael. But would you have drawn so deeply on your own resources when you encountered other Beings if you had been accompanied by such as I?"

I shrug helplessly. What can I say?

"Look!" The Shepherd's voice is commanding, and as I look into the window, I am falling . . . falling . . .

. . . into a future Earth probability. To my immense relief, the Shepherd is at my side. "We are invisible to other people, Michael. We are shadows of light, observers, unseen and unrealized."

"This happens often, doesn't it?" I ask on a surge of insight. "Other Beings often drop in to see how things are shaping up on three-dimensional Earth."

The Shepherd is amused. "Yes, as a matter of fact they do." He paused. "And not always for your benefit."

I feel alarmed by his words. "What do you mean?"

"You will see," he replies, dismissing it.

Looking around, I see that we are on a farm, even though it is different from any farm of my experience.

"I suppose this is no coincidence, is it? I mean, I always seem to learn so much from Nature, either on a farm or in the more wild environments."

"This is your way, Michael. You are not particularly receptive to people, but very open to Nature. A metaphysical Nature is your path." The Shepherd gestures around us expansively. "So, what do you think of this? Does it appeal?"

I shudder. We are standing on the edge of a small spinney of low, spreading trees. We could be in England, for it has a familiar feeling to me, but if so, it is a very changed England. The farm is obviously a dairy farm. The dairy is close to where we are standing, and, unobserved, the Shepherd and I enter the large building. It is an obscenity. I look toward the Shepherd to see how he feels about this, but if he is feeling any disgust it is not apparent on his benign features. I look at the cows—if that is what they can be called—and shudder in revulsion. Each cow is no more than a biological unit in a very large, milking, feeding, life-support machine. The cows are grotesque. They each have a head, mouth, body, and a huge gross udder, but none of them has eyes, ears, or legs. Each sad, unhappy animal is housed in a large container, constantly hooked into the machine. Liquid food is fed into them via a couple of tubes, while the milk they produce is constantly drawn from them through one large central teat in the udder.

I stare at the shepherd, appalled. "Is this real?" I choke. "This abomination is absolutely disgusting!"

The Shepherd shrugs, looking sad. "This is considered the pinnacle of advanced milk production in this reality. It is certainly happening."

I recall my earlier vision in the sphere over the river, when I was shown the giants and their horrendous genetic experimentation, and I realize that the arrogant desire to manipulate and subjugate Nature is still with this future humanity. In fact, it is obviously finding a whole new expression. Remembering where it finally led the giants, I shudder.

"How can you allow it?" I ask indignantly. "This is absolutely gross—the ultimate degradation of an animal. And it's dangerous."

He looks at me levelly. "Michael, this is choice. The farmers involved in this method of milk production have deliberately chosen it, while all those who drink the milk have inadvertently chosen it. However, even in this reality, there are those who resist such methods."

As he speaks, a couple of men dressed in white, sterile overalls, walk toward us, deeply engaged in conversation. They stand close by us, watching one of the poor deformed cows. After a while, one of the men steps toward it, and with a small instrument looking like a pen, presses it on the side of the cow's head. There is a sharp hiss, and the cow shudders, going suddenly limp. Briskly, the two men disconnect the cow, swinging the container out across the driveway so that the carcass can be dumped into a mobile trolley that has just trundled up. Moments later, another trolley arrives, and another slightly smaller cow unit is attached to the horrific machine. The whole process has taken maybe ten minutes.

The Shepherd and I follow the trolley containing the dead cow unit into another large building containing a number of sealed, yet transparent, vats. The cow unit is dumped onto a conveyer and quickly deposited into a vat. As we watch, the cow unit begins to melt rapidly.

"Is that acid?" I ask, shocked.

"No," the Shepherd replies. "The vat contains specially produced enzymes and bacteria. The cow unit is in the process of becoming food for the other cow units."

I am appalled, silenced by sadness. Together, we walk among other vats. Through the transparent sides, I see that new cow units are being grown in a synthetic biological imitation of a womb, and held in a thick, jellylike nutrient suspension until almost full grown and needed. I feel sick.

"Would you like to see a hospital of this reality?" the Shepherd asks me, with a level gaze.

"No!" I gasp vehemently. "This is no place that I will ever live. Besides, I don't think I could handle seeing the human equivalent of this violation. Is this the outcome of genetic manipulation?"

"One outcome, Michael, just one reality of it. In this reality, human ethics, integrity, and spiritual values are given no consideration."

"Are there reality frames involving genetic manipulation where the outcome is different?" I ask.

"Oh yes, very different. There are reality frames where genetic engineering is married to the highest expression of moral and spiritual principles."

"And you are saying that all these realities occupy the same space?"

"Exactly."

"Sort of like a loaf of sliced bread, with all the different slices making up the whole loaf?"

"That says it nicely."

"Is it possible then to travel from one reality/slice to another reality/slice in the whole loaf/Greater Reality?"

"Of course."

"How?"

"By changing your focus, by acting out your new focus, and living the truth of that focus. This will create an expansion in consciousness that will eventually take you into a Greater Reality."

"So this must be an anyway shift? I mean a person can shift into a reality that is more spiritual, with higher ideals and expressions, or into a reality that is base and more gross?"

"Yes, people do it all the time. However, to change your frame of reality requires a more drastic approach."

My insight is blossoming as I follow it. "Am I correct in assuming that in the process we call life and living we can expand and enrich our current reality, but when a more drastic change in reality is reached, we do it through the process we call death and dying?"

The Shepherd looks pleased. "Absolutely right."

"So death may well be our greatest triumph of change and growth?"

"It can be that, yes. That is always the potential. But it can also be no more than a recycling of conditioned sameness. Choice, Michael, choice. And it takes choice just to choose! It is far easier to stay with sameness than risk the choice of change."

"And yet sameness equates as suffering," I add.

The Shepherd nods. "But change means risk, and most humans tend to avoid risks. Even those who work with danger, or take sporting risks, shy away from the risk of leaving consensus reality—of stretching, expanding, and growing in consciousness."

"And of losing the approval of consensus reality. Which equates to becoming a misfit, a social outcast."

"That is the way of it, Michael."

I gaze at my light body and spread my arms wide. "So why am I here in this incredible reality? What is the real purpose of all this?"

The Shepherd gazes into my eyes. "Love, Michael. It's all about Love. Both humanity and the planet Earth resonate to the vibration of Love. Love is the creative force, the power of Change and growth. Love is your natural creative expression, your path to Godhood, but you are required to choose it. This *is* your human process. Anything less than Love is very definitely less!" He opens his arms in a gesture that embraces the farm and the pitiful cow units.

I shudder. The absence of love in this awful place carries its own horrid message of hopelessness and despair.

"Michael, use your deeper senses as we walk across the fields and through the spinney. Attune with Nature," the Shepherd instructs.

Perhaps unwisely, I turn my focus of attunement toward the cow units and recoil in shock. Each cow unit, in both the vats and in the machine, is shrouded in heavy shadow. Instead of the normal life-force illumination around a living creature, there is a field of shadowy energy, heavy with distortion and discord.

"This is dreadful," I gasp. "I've never experienced anything like it. I shudder to think of the causal effect that humanity is sowing here. It will be a harvest of paramount misery and suffering."

The Shepherd is grim. "This certainly represents a poor choice when it comes to learning about life, Michael, but the lessons will be learned. Pain and suffering are harsh teachers, but remarkably effective. Come, let us walk away from all this depression."

We walk toward a field of green abundance, where an

ovoid, silvery, car-sized machine is cutting the lush vegetation with the smooth, gliding ease of a vacuum cleaner sliding over a plush green carpet. The Shepherd drops back a couple of steps—deliberately withdrawing his influence from my experience—while I walk into a field of some unknown vegetation that is growing faster than anything I have ever seen. Even as it is harvested, it is visibly growing. Staring, I go onto my hands and knees to see how it is cut, and learn that it is not cut; somehow, the plant stems are biologically separated as the machine passes over them. Physically, this seems a great advance, but the vibration of energy from the plants is a message of harsh discord.

I sit down and relax, focusing *into* Nature, and the reason for the discord becomes obvious: There are no Nature spirits here at all. From the greatest of the Nature Beings to the tiniest of Nature spirits that I encountered earlier, not a single representative is here. There is nothing but genetically altered, biologically rampant plant growth. Each plant is as captive and manipulated as the cow units. They are genetically induced and chemically stimulated to produce growth, and their container is an enslaved environment where the ecosystem is captive to rampant greed. The discord that is so apparent to me is obviously not felt by the human violators. However, the discord of this green food is fed into the cow units to combine with their discord and distress. The resulting accumulated discordance—made into a wide range of dairy food products—is then fed into a system that ends up in human bodies. What an irony! The society that condones and produces this unnatural discord reaps the harvest of its own misery.

I turn to the Shepherd. "I still don't want to see the hospitals," I tell him, "but I bet anything that they are always full."

The Shepherd makes a curious gesture, and we are standing on the sidewalk of a dark, brooding city. "I respect your reluctance to enter a hospital, but you should have a brief glimpse of city life. Cities similar to this are home to the overwhelming masses."

It takes me a while to understand my perception of the city. We are standing on a street, but above us there are other streets in a sequence of tiers, and below, still more. With a wave of his hand, the Shepherd and I drift downward into dirtier and more debased slums. The really odd thing is that each level of complex streets seems to be at ground level, but I am learning that these are literally multi-tiered ghettos, or structures of society. This is based not on differing nationalities, but on income, money, or, as it is known in this reality, credits.

The buildings are immense, towering as shades of dark grime to the streets above. I get the impression that the buildings are both the habitats of the people and the support structure for the streets. The streets appear to be held on a network of surprisingly slim metallic girders, strung between the buildings. "How is this possible?" I ask. "I would have thought that the weight of such huge buildings would have fractured the concrete in the lower levels, destabilizing them. And the iron framework that supports the streets looks too flimsy to hold the weight."

The Shepherd smiles grimly. "Even though the principles of real Love slumber in this reality zone, technology grows apace. A way was found not only to improve the strength of concrete, but to build in a certain flexibility. There is no limit to the possible height and weight of a building in this reality. Equally, iron and plastic were melded, each taking on the best qualities of the other. This material has tremendous strength and is almost immune to climate, acids, and natural deterioration."

Gazing around me at the squalor and grime, I sigh. "And this is the best that they can do with such advanced technology?"

The Shepherd shrugs. "When the highest principles of humanity are sacrificed, everyone becomes exploited."

The people around us are reasonably normal to look at, except they all seem young. "Where are the aged?" I ask.

His smile is sad. "At these lower levels of society, there are rarely any aged people. There is no welfare, no charity—only survival. The hopeless, injured, sick, and infirm take a tiny painless pill. That's it, the end—for a while."

Few people are alone; mostly they travel around in groups. The most basic transport looks like a motorized skateboard of varying sizes, except the motor is about the size of a football and silent. Some carry half a dozen people, some have one person, but they seem to swerve in and around a certain set parameter in an alarming manner. It is cold, but people wear only thin, almost transparent clothing cut into an incredible array of colors and styles. Obviously the material has some really remarkable insulation ability, for although the people may be unhappy and highly stressed, quite clearly, they are not cold.

We come to a stop in our downward drift on the lowest level of the streets—ground level. A stench hangs in the air, held by a permanent mist. At the sunniest time of the day, it becomes a mellow twilight, before the shadows creep out to envelop the shame in darkness. It is dreadful.

"Do people actually live in this? When is this reality future? I know it is a framework of Now, but it also has a linear reality. When is that?"

"About three hundred years down your time track will see this all in place. You have to understand that each person creates his or her own reality. This is one outcome of a consensus reality of greed and indifference. While greed and indifference are held in the human consciousness, they must find a physical expression. This is a principle of life."

"I want to leave this place. I find it hard to believe that such a future is possible." I look around and shudder, aware of very few people. "If the inhabitants take a lethal pill when they are too sick to continue, how is it that there are any hospitals in this reality?"

"Hospitals are for those with sufficient credit," the Shepherd tells me, "while the pills are freely available to the poor. You are seeing nothing more than a fleeting overview of all this. War as you know it has been abolished in this society, for practically everyone is another's adversary. Living and surviving are a daily battle—the ultimate war. This reality draws the worst from each person, rather than the best." He smiles at my dismay. "Hard to imagine?"

I nod. "As with the cow units, this reminds me in some ways of the giants in a past era. This reality has the same elements of cruelty and indifference."

"Very true. Those giants were a pre-race of the present

humanity, but they still continue within another reality frame of Now. They . . ."

I cut in. "You mean in another slice in the loaf?"

"Yes. Human life is an expression of consciousness. The causal discord of the giants is still being expressed in humanity, but this is not everyone's reality. If you choose love, then love is your reality. If you do not choose love, then your conditioning will determine your reality."

"Does it ever end?" I ask.

The Shepherd smiles enigmatically. "Did it ever really begin? Come, let me show you the other aspect of this city before we depart."

We float rapidly upward, and I count six street levels before we come into obvious wealth and affluence. This level is amazing. Beyond the streets it is open parkland, with mountains to be seen in the distance. Birds abound, with rainbows arcing across a deep blue sky. "Wow! This is better," I gasp, delighted.

"Attune with the Nature you see around you," the Shepherd suggests. "You might get a surprise."

I focus into the light force of Nature—and nothing! I can see an abundant Nature all around me, but my attunement reveals nothing. I frown at the Shepherd's smile, puzzled.

"I suppose common sense should tell me that you cannot landscape a high-rise space, but it looks like a beautiful ground-level Botanical Park."

"It's all holographs—an elaborate illusion," he tells me. We walk over to a courtyard overflowing with red and pink roses as they clamber along a balustrade. Reaching out, I touch the blossom of a rose and feel its coolness. I even inhale its fragrance, but my finer, attuned senses indicate that it is not a real rose. The illusion contains a high degree of physical substance, but it is somehow unreal.

"How can a rose be unreal, an illusion, yet have substance?"

"It's a form of virtual reality—a misnomer, if ever there was one," the Shepherd replies. "It is so well contrived that only those who understand the principles involved are able to detect the false from the real. Most people here believe that all this"—the Shepherd indicates around us with a wave of his hands—"is real. They are deluded, unable to discern real life from fabricated illusion. So much for brain-form patterns and their deliberate manipulation."

Slowly, I am comprehending the implications of this amazing delusion. "What an insidious form of control! The people on the lower levels are more in touch with reality than these poor souls."

The Shepherd's smile is whimsical. "What is reality?"

I open my mouth to reply, then close it. What indeed?

Together, the Shepherd and I walk among the people. As before, on the lower levels, I cannot understand the language. It seems to have a touch of English mixed with other languages. However, I can understand what people say, for I hear them on a telepathic level that is beyond all language—the inner voice. I get the impression that the people on this level are all drugged happy, whereas only a few were obviously on drugs on the lower levels. Here, everyone seems to be on a permanent high, their fixed smile hiding an acute inner emptiness. Physically, everyone is beautiful and wearing very little clothing. Wispy materials that reflect a different color with every turn and twist of the body seem the most popular choice. The material is transparent, yet the colors artfully defeat the eye according to the whim of the wearer in what is evidently a seductive and tantalizing fashion.

Elderly people are to be seen everywhere, vital and healthy in appearance, while the children are in large groups, supervised by an adult. Most of the children wear nothing, comfortable in a stable, permanent warmth.

"I suppose, all things considered, that this is better than the lower levels," I say.

"You think so." The Shepherd nods toward a slightly more corpulent man as he walks by. "That is the Cowmaster — using a cynical term — overseeing his human/cow units. Even if it is a less demanding system than the milking machine, these people are just as surely being sucked dry."

"I don't understand. It looks better than down below."

The Shepherd smiles a tight, brief smile, his eyes flashing dangerously. "The lower levels are left to their own devices. Most of them are the rebels, the troublemakers, yet they are the saving grace of this reality frame. It is from them and their growing shame at their own callous indifference that change is precipitated into this reality."

The Shepherd looks up. "Come. See where that anger is directed."

We ascend swiftly, two unseen ghosts from two different realities, moving through the ethers of energy that hold all realities apart — and together — as One. Soon, we stand on the highest level, overlooking a very changed scene. Here is opulence. We appear to be surrounded by mansions and castles spun from the threads of a rainbow. They occupy the space that on every other level is taken by the vast buildings that tower, up and up, on each side of the streets. On the level we just left, the buildings were hidden by virtual reality. Maybe this is the same; it is the only explanation possible.

The Shepherd knows my shared thoughts. "Actually, no. The buildings have ended here. However, they are the frame upon which all this stands. The true land is obviously far below us, yet, with their technology, they have created enough synthetic soil to fabricate a replica of Earth conditions in the style that appeals to them. Enough to say that much of what you see here is real, with a little help from virtual reality. It is enhanced to create the illusion of great space and distance, as though on the ground, yet, in reality, it is not as large as it appears. Here, in the terms of credits, is wealth beyond reckoning."

A family group appears—two children and a woman. I cannot tell if the children are boys or girls, for they appear disturbingly sexless. However, like the woman, they have such radiant, healthy energy that they are enshrouded in a visible aura of shimmering color.

"Are they Gods or what?" I ask, awed.

"They are no more and no less Gods than every human Being is. What you see is the result of genetic manipulation and chromosome flushing. The consequence is spectacular in physical appearance and longevity."

"I bet this costs a heap to maintain."

"Almost nothing is impossible here if credits can make it happen, but there is another, more demanding price to pay. Michael, what would you say is the overall expression of this reality?"

"That's easy. In a word, discord. Overwhelming, never-ending, unremitting discord. And that means suffering. Oceans of suffering."

The Shepherd points dramatically. "Look! Observe what I reveal."

One of the nearby palaces seems to get closer and closer, but I quickly realize that my perspective is being altered. I am now able to see clearly into a huge room and to observe the people in it. People! Only some of them are human! Mixed and mingled among the couple of dozen normal humans are a number of short, gray-skinned humanoids. Aided by the Shepherd, my insight expands, and I understand what I am seeing. The Gray Ones have a humanoid form, are around five feet tall, and have blurred features. I realize that this is deliberate, but the humans see them as normal people. I am really shocked when I perceive that, on a psychic level, the Gray Ones feed off human misery and suffering. In this reality, there are no human winners. All are losers. Everyone! Not just some of the people and a besieged Nature. Somehow, this whole reality is contrived, controlled, and manipulated by a parasitic race of Beings. I feel an overwhelming sadness.

"That is not quite true, Michael. The Gray Ones did not create this; they are merely opportunists. There are no winners here. The Gray Ones do not win, for they are victims of their own most base and negative desires. This is the way of life. Your linear, three-dimensional reality is unendingly causal. You can only live within the reality frame of your own causality. If greed and indifference are within your consciousness, then eventually you must experience their outworking, their effect.

"I have shown you this for a reason. Your insight into the timeless Reality you are experiencing will be shared. This is part of your purpose in life. You are involved in a process that began a long time ago—in linear terms. There are people in your everyday reality who are ready to move beyond the limitations of a mundane consensus reality, progressing toward the birthright of their human divinity.

"This reality we are visiting is but one consensus reality among many. This one is almost, not quite, devoid of the expression of real Love."

It is a very unhappy place. I sigh. How ironic, to be in a loveless reality, when each and every human is a Being of Light and Love, manifest into physical form?

As my thoughts end, we drift away, leaving that blighted place. We seem to flow through other frames of reality, for occasional glimpses of otherness touch my perception, yet in only moments the Shepherd and I are again in his craft, standing in the familiar room of mystic windows and gazing into what is now an opaque glass panel.

I stare wonderingly at the blank panel. "Did all that really happen?" I ask. "Did we really travel into a future reality, or did you induce a dream projection?"

The Shepherd's whimsical smile is back. "Do you mean

was it a real reality, a dream reality, or an illusion? I ask you again, Michael, what is reality?"

I think carefully before I reply. "Er . . . reality is the experience of now, in whatever way, manner, form, or dimension it takes place. Reality has no limits . . ." I stop as my insight reveals more. "Reality is the expression of consciousness, however that may manifest. An event that is experienced on a three-dimensional level will be a very different reality from the same event experienced on a higher dimensional plane. Reality is not the event, but the experience of it, and the experience differs with everybody. Therefore, we each create our own reality." My eyes open ever wider as I follow my insight. "If we are open to a greater expression of life, we expand our reality of life, and as we expand our reality of life, so we eventually cross the metaphysical threshold into a truly limitless Reality. All this is determined by each one of us."

The Shepherd nods. "Very good. If only you could be as expansive and all-embracing as your words."

I frown. "I happen to think that I'm doing okay."

He looks at me, still nodding. "Yes, I agree, you are. However, the reality is that when you leave this timeless realm you will remember approximately ten percent of your whole experience. You will retain only the ten percent that you are physically writing even as we talk. Even that, you will accept only because you will not be able to deny what you have written. Despite this, you will even fight against your own words. You are at the stage of entering the threshold. Part of you is held, fixed and stuck in a consensus reality, while another part is moving into a Greater metaphysical Reality. Sadly, these two major aspects of you will be in conflict."

"Which part of me will win?"

"That is not for me to say. The conflict will be very basic—self-denial versus self-acceptance. In its many different guises, this is the overall conflict of humanity. If you overcome your conflict—and nothing less than Self-Realization will accomplish this, then you will know your purpose in this physical incarnation. Each word that you are now writing as you physically sit in your bed is a primer. If you make that quantum leap in consciousness—crossing the threshold—the skeleton of words you have written will become fully fleshed, and *all* your experiences in this realm will be remembered as a happening of Now."

"Suppose I do remember everything; is it allowed?"

"Of course you are allowed. The choice to forget is yours. It is the only way you see of being able to deal with the immensity of this metaphysical experience. The part of you that clings to a consensus reality will be so overwhelmed with the whole memory that you could be emotionally traumatized. The probability is that you will not be able to deal with it."

"Suppose I don't attain Self-Realization?"

"If you focus on such possibilities, you will ensure that you do not, at least in this incarnation."

An incredible, scary resolve sweeps through me. "In my physical terms, I am forty years of age," I tell the Shepherd. "I vow that I will be Awake and Self-Realized by the time I am fifty, or dead. I will not continue my life longer than that in the consensus-reality illusions."

"This might not be very wise, Michael, but if you mean it—and I perceive that, on a soul level, you do—you have just invoked a very powerful catalytic focus. Be very careful and aware with your thoughts, for you have now created a condition where they will either set you Free—or kill you."

For a few moments, I am stunned by my own rash action. In some deep inner center, I know that what I have invoked will come to pass, one way or the other, yet I feel no fear. The decision has been made, and I have a knowing that I cannot unmake it. I cannot back out, nor do I want to.

As we walk toward another window panel, my thoughts turn back to the Gray Ones. In some deep submerged part of me, I have the feeling that I have encountered these Beings before, but I have no memory of it.

"Just who are those unpleasant Gray characters?"

The Shepherd's smile indicates that he has expected the question. "They are three-dimensional Beings who for many ages have fallen by the wayside of spiritual evolution. They have learned how to travel space—as you call it—promoting greed and misery in other intelligent life forms that are susceptible to their coercion. However, they are also part of the Divine Creative Principle, just as you and I are. Imagine the opportunity they create for those other Beings to let go of their fears and negativity and consciously grow. In this way, the Gray Ones are also very powerful agents of change."

"Where do they come from?"

"They are stuck in a very negative realm of reality."

"That doesn't tell me where they're from."

"I hesitate to get you bogged down in fixed ideas of where is home. That is as silly as suggesting that humanity is from Earth. You are Beings of infinite Reality, and Earth is no more than a temporary classroom in your journey of life. The linear time you spend on Earth is a single drop in a whole ocean of timelessness. Does this then make Earth your home?"

"Hmmm. I take it then that the Gray Ones are sort of wandering, high-tech, cosmic thugs?"

The Shepherd laughs, his head thrown back. Finally, wiping tears of mirth from his eyes, he beckons me over to another panel. Chuckling, he indicates another scene. "Is this more to your liking?"

Once again, I am looking down onto and into the city that I saw earlier. There are great multicolored domes that seem to change color as I watch and several vast buildings that are an incredible array of silvery pyramidal angles arranged in an intersected cluster of multiple tetrahedrons. Not only is it very impressive to look at, but the city emanates a powerful atmosphere of peace and tranquility.

"This is a lot better than that other place," I comment.

"Same time frame, different reality."

"It's hard to understand that each time/frame has other different realities."

"This time/frame reality is in sharp contrast to the one we visited," the Shepherd tells me. "They are so extremely different that they cannot exist together in one frame."

"Sort of like oil and water," I suggest.

His deep blue eyes hold mine. "Exactly. The difference, however, is in consciousness; physical form here is similar to that other reality, although more sensitized and refined. In your present time/frame, consensus reality holds all the middle ground of the general population. Consensus reality varies, of course, among different nations, cultures, and religions. Trying to match the consensus reality of this huge conglomerate mismatch is the catalyst for most of your wars. It inevitably leads to conflict rather than cooperation. It is sad that humans invariably focus on their few differences rather than on their many similarities.

"However, within all this there are those people who plumb the depths of depravity and cruelty, victimizing many of the weak and helpless. Equally, there are others who rise far above all conflict and differences, finding the deepest Love and compassion for all humanity. Inadvertently, the expression of these two extremes of human consciousness creates whole new frames of reality, for these people no longer fit even in the periphery of a consensus reality."

"So the reality frame we have just visited is the negative extreme of human expression—the sinners—while this"—I indicate the city in the window panel—"is the reality frame of the compassionate, loving people—the saints. Yet each reality occupies the same time/frame?"

The Shepherd laughs at my humor. "I know you are not serious, Michael, but I must remind you that every human is a divine Being of Light and Love. Losing touch with this state of consciousness is not evil, any more than retaining such a focus is good. Good and evil are descriptions based on judgment, and judgment has not served humanity at all well. Discern always, but never judge."

216

"What's the difference?"

The Shepherd's smile becomes mischievous. "Let me use sex as an example. You are walking down the corridor in a hotel on your way to your room. A door opens and a beautiful scantily clad girl beckons you in. In the room, you can see several naked people engaged in group sex. The girl tells you they need another man. If you say, 'No way, what you are doing is wrong and wicked,' you have made a judgment. However, if you say, 'No thanks, I prefer not to be involved,' you have discerned for yourself, but made no judgment on the other people."

"And if I join in?"

Laughing, the Shepherd replies, "Then, perhaps, you didn't judge or discern. Whichever you choose, neither is right nor wrong. You sow cause, and you reap effect."

Peering into the city as the view presents an ever-changing panorama, I ask hopefully, "Are we going to visit this reality?"

"Of course. The same rules apply: We are disembodied in this reality, just auras of Light. Now, look deeply into the city."

I do so, expecting that we will be instantly there, but instead . . .

. . . I am floating and drifting through the panel and up, ever up, in a dreamy sensation of light, peace, and joy. The sensation is powerful and pronounced.

"How can we be floating up when the city is below us?" I ask, in a blissful daze.

"Surely you realize that this is neither up nor down, but through," the Shepherd replies.

I do not understand, but I feel too relaxed to care. "This is different, somehow slower, more joyous—both more real and yet unreal at the same time," I say dreamily.

The Shepherd has lost most of his bodily definition, appearing as a haze of golden light in human shape. "Your perception is more acute now; thus, your experience is expanded. We are traveling exactly as before," he replies.

"But we were there almost instantly last time."

"I repeat, your perception is expanded; thus, you experience more of the reality, instead of blocking it out. Remember, as you change yourself, you change your reality experience."

"Wow! I must use 'block out' automatically."

"Indeed you do. It is part of the human condition."

Any sadness I might feel for the human condition is lost in my increasing feeling of joy. "How strange. It's only now that I feel such joy that I'm aware of the corresponding vibration of misery in our visit to the other reality zone."

"Exactly. Your initial reaction was to subconsciously block it out because it was so unpleasant, but you were unable to maintain that block. You are more open and receptive now because you are responding to the energy of Love within this reality."

"So the aura of human energy affects us, even without any personal interaction?"

"Very much. The human energy field is a powerhouse

that can be felt across infinity. Humanity is learning how to develop, expand, and express that power. In the previous reality we visited, the people are closed to that energy, and even closed off from one another, yet they remain victims of their own energy creation. Here, the overall energy field is nourishing for the soul, even without personal contact. This is what you are now feeling."

The faintly shimmering golden glow that is the Shepherd is achingly beautiful. "Do I appear to you in the way that you appear to me?" I ask hopefully.

"According to your viewpoint, you are less defined than before, but to me, you appear as more truly your Self. Self is beauty beyond imagining."

During our silent communication, we have drifted into the streets of the magnificent city. I am immediately aware of the absolute difference between this city of a future reality and the City of Living Glass that I visited earlier. This city has been lovingly built and created, but that other City is *alive*—an expression of a vast and aware consciousness.

I look around me, captivated. What I assume to be streets are obviously not for traffic. There is no traffic. No cars or buses or delivery trucks, not even bicycles. But there are lots of people. The street we are in is lined with trees unlike any I have ever seen. The foliage is sprucelike, with short, thick needles of glittering silver. I would normally assume the trees to be fakes, so odd are they, but the life force emanating from them is too strong to deny. Although I am not physical, my sense of touch reveals that, unlike spruce, these needles are soft and fleshy. In some ways they look like spray-painted Christmas trees, except that as I look I realize that the needles are gently moving. As though being stroked by an invisible hand along the branches, the needles bend in a rhythmic ripple of motion.

"This is amazing!" I exclaim.

"It is the result of genetic intervention. In this case, the geneticists have set up some very complex instrumentation that feeds the response of the plant into a computer. They experiment with certain "biological suggestions," the plant registering either its discord or accord with this. In this frame of reality, the geneticists develop the plant only with its total approval. Some geneticists have become so skilled that they are able to bypass the instruments, attuning directly into the consciousness of the plant. As you can feel, these trees both approve of and enjoy their movement in physical form."

"Why do I get the feeling that the DNA of sea anemones may be involved?" I ask.

"As is apparent, they are involved," the Shepherd replies. "And would it surprise you to know that they found a way to allow the sea anemones to branch out into tree-type expressions?"

I look at him in mock surprise. "What's this, a pun from a cosmic Being? Whatever next?" As we laugh, I realize that there is an effervescent quality in the atmosphere of the city, almost mildly intoxicating. Even the Shepherd is not immune to the sense of fun that it invokes.

For the first time, I really *know* what he meant when he spoke about the two extremes of expression in our human consciousness. This is the absolute opposite to the earlier frame of reality we visited. It is only now that I realize just why we visited that other frame. The Shepherd knew that by experiencing that earlier frame I would be able to fully appreciate this one. Expansion by contrast!

"Is there any way from that misery frame to this joyous frame in a single lifetime?" I ask.

"No. You would have to die to that negative expression of consciousness to incarnate into this reality. Even then, it would be a prodigious quantum leap in consciousness."

"But possible?"

"Yes."

"There is always hope," I say brightly.

"I would prefer that you say, 'There is always Love.'"

"Oh, why?" I ask, puzzled.

"Because the expression of hope can be quite static. The expression of Love is creative and moving; it promotes change. Hope tends to look outside for help and waits; Love looks within and finds the power of Self."

"Thank you. That's something I definitely need to practice. It opens up a whole new realm of exploration."

"It does indeed, and that exploration is all within Self. Everything you have ever needed in life is always with you. All humans hold all the wisdom, capacity, capability, and potential of their divinity. It is all in your own consciousness, awaiting you."

An image comes to my mind. "It sounds rather like a man crawling through a dry, blazing hot desert, looking for water. Strapped to his back is a canteen of cool, delicious water, but he cannot see it, or is unable to acknowledge that it is with him."

"Something like that, except that it is impossible to ever

lose the canteen, or empty it, or despoil the water," the Shepherd adds.

"That analogy comes to mind so easily because I am one of those in the desert," I say gloomily.

"But you are here, now," the Shepherd replies gently, "and this is no desert."

A moment later, a peal of laughter strips away my gloom, and I spin around to see a group of nearby teenagers. To my astonishment, they are watching us. They look at me with some curiosity, but it is clear that they regard the Shepherd with a familiar Love and reverence.

"They can see us," I gasp, blurting the obvious.

The Shepherd chuckles, acknowledging them. "People born into this reality are very developed spiritually. These 'teenagers' are very aware souls. They can see me in exactly the way you are seeing me. The difference is that while your abilities are being enhanced by me, these young people are using their own ability."

"But we were invisible before," I protest.

"Michael, can you imagine those other poor souls seeing anything beyond their own contained reality? They have walls of fear around them; these people are opened by Love."

Put like that, it seems so obvious!

All the teenagers have a golden-tan skin color, and very little clothing. Curiously, their clothing is very similar to the people of that other reality—almost sheer and rippling with color as they move and breathe. Despite the film of rippling color, most of the teenagers appear almost nude, and it seems as natural as breathing. Without exception, they are all beautiful. They glow with exuberant health, eyes shining, bright with the sheer enthusiasm of life. Intelligence and alert awareness radiate from them as a tangible aura.

Waving, they beckon for us to follow them. "Can we communicate with them?" I ask the Shepherd. "They obviously know you."

"I can communicate with them in the same way that I communicate with you. We are well acquainted."

The group of teenagers are stepping into an energy band of colored light that runs down the center of the street. In some ways it resembles a dense rainbow that simply follows the contours of the street, merging into other similar rainbows where the streets intersect. As soon as they step into it, the whole group lifts a few inches off the ground, laughing and playful as they gesture for us to accompany them. Oddly, several other people traveling in the same energy band are going much faster, moving past the teenagers in what appears to be a collision-proof system of travel.

"Try it," the Shepherd suggests.

Needing no urging, I float into the stream of colored energy. Instantly, a field of force seems to hold me, and I am aware that it will respond to the mental projection of how and where I wish to travel—fast or slow, and wherever in the city I want to go. I project the thought of following our new friends, and with no sensation of movement, I am instantly with their group.

"This sure beats our public transportation."

By the time I have finished my inane remark, we are in

a completely different area, standing alongside this remarkable conveyer. How we got here, and disembarked, with no sensation of movement or any awareness of traveling, I have no idea. We are in a large Park, with flowering shrubs and trees landscaped into complementary groups of color. Instead of grass as a lawn, the whole area is covered in some creeping, prostrate plant that is new to me. Its foliage is soft, like that of a tiny-leafed fern; surprisingly, it is aromatic, reminiscent of lemon. I suspect that it never needs mowing. Within the Park is a very large, dome-shaped building, rising to a modest peak in the center of the dome. The energy in the Park is tranquil, yet very focused. It occurs to me that different areas of the city and environs have deliberately induced fields of energy.

As the group of young teenagers beckons to me, I follow them into the impressive white dome. The inside is strange. Above my head there is a baffling structure of crystal in the peak of the dome, with what appears to be a large carousel of low glass coffins directly beneath it. I turn to the Shepherd for an explanation.

"Michael, just watch."

As many other young people stream into the building, the group with us is getting into the structures I erroneously thought of as coffins. On closer inspection, I see that they are more like individual cubicles/beds on the huge carousel. Each one is made from a clear, transparent material like soft plastic, which molds and adjusts itself to fit the person who occupies it.

A woman wearing a light, white tunic is supervising. She bows slightly to the Shepherd, a look of profound respect on her face, and she smiles at me. As the teenagers settle into their cubicles, lying flat on their backs, an indicator flicks alight on a panel near the supervisor. Soon, the panel is fully lit up, all cubicles occupied and ready. Turning to the panel, the woman makes a number of gestures that are obviously commands. The crystal structure high above at the peak of the dome lights up, beaming a different color of light onto different sections of the carousel. At a guess, there may have been two to three hundred teenagers on the carousel. Next, the carousel begins to turn very slowly, while the teenagers relax, eyes closed, seemingly asleep.

Stepping closer, I see that an opaque, helmetlike apparatus covers the head and face of each occupant. Completely baffled, I look at the Shepherd in perplexity.

"This is weird!"

He smiles. "They are students."

Suddenly, it is all so overwhelmingly obvious. This is a school in this reality. Instead of learning by rote, information is fed directly into their brains and minds while they are relaxed in an alpha/theta brain wave.

The Shepherd knows of my sudden comprehension, attuned to my broadcast thoughts.

"There is much more to it than that. The carousel moves the students through different colors, each one stimulating a certain response. The crystal through which the light shines is programmed, rather like a supermind that directly connects and communicates with the student through vibration. Every part of the student is involved, not only the brain. Each cell of the body is intimately involved. In this process, the students *experience* what they are learning. Each physical sense perception is involved, while the psyche is metaphysically stimulated. This is why they are able to see you and me, even though we are not physical. Their awareness is such that they can even see and hear through their *skin* while under the influence of this educational capacitor."

"Capacitor! Does that mean that there is electricity involved?"

"Certainly. The crystal generates an electrical current that is transferred via the vibration of color directly into the body electric of the student. As you know, even the pattern of your thought is electrical."

"This sure as hell beats the punish-and-condemn method that was forced onto me," I say enviously.

"In your reality frame, you are just beginning to develop what you call 'virtual reality.' Using that definition, these students are having a virtual reality experience, although it is far beyond anything that the people of your reality have devised. These students are not passively hooked into information. Within the parameters of their lesson, they are able to choose what they experience, fully participating in their learning."

"How long is school each day?"

"Approximately three hours. During that time, through direct virtual experience, they assimilate considerably more than in a month of the method you experienced."

"A month!" I cry out. "That's impossible."

The Shepherd faces me calmly. "At six years of age, these students have learned almost all there is to know about the human body and the way to maintain optimum health. Everything, inside and out."

"Perhaps that is why they are all so physically perfect." It is true. I noticed as the students arrived that although hair color and eye color vary a great deal, all the teenagers have the golden-tan skin, and they are mostly slim and quite tall. Without exception, they *all* radiate vibrant health.

"It's rather daunting to be faced by such perfection," I comment. "Are all the adults like this?"

"Michael, remember this is a time/frame of a future reality. Do not compare these people with your present humanity. You are living in a time when the great potential of many brilliant individuals is suppressed. Your people are stricken with disease, war, famine, and suffering on a level that rivals anything in your historical past. All of your true geniuses who develop the means for holistic health and a global abundance of food are persecuted, ridiculed, restrained, and controlled by rampant corporate greed and consensus reality. However, as always, the greater the suppression, the greater the resulting explosion.

"What do you mean?"

"You live in a time of great cataclysm, a time of an explosive upheaval in consciousness. This can be seen environmentally in the unprecedented speed of change. The times you live in will be the determining factor of your next reality frame. Some of your humanity will incarnate into the reality that we visited earlier; some will incarnate here. The big majority, however, will probably incarnate back into a reality frame that is a continuation of your present mode."

"How is this decided?"

"By how you live your life. By your individual state of consciousness. It is determined not by what you know, but by the degree of Love you are able to express in your daily life. Love that has no cause, motivation, or conditions — just a need to express your highest ideals and principles."

"I know where the multimillionaire manipulators and prime movers will go," I say, thinking of that other place.

"Do you? Or is this a judgment of right and wrong? All that is happening in your present time/frame — from the most gross/negative to the ultra-positive — is a reflection of the *whole* human consciousness of that frame. There is truly no right and wrong, good or bad; there is only the individual expressions of fear/deny or Love/accept, and all the shades in between that determine the eternal Now of each individual within the Whole. Neither innocence nor guilt, nor judgment and blame has any place within this; it is *all* self-determined."

"Yes, I spoke rashly. I do know better," I amend apologetically. "It's so easy to slip into judging."

"Michael, in this reality there are no hospitals, no disease, no sickness. Any touch of discord is detected in the body aura and treated before it manifests into the physical. These people of what you term tomorrow are the product of your today. This is your human potential."

Although the Shepherd appears as a glowing, slightly nebulous angelic figure in this reality, I relate to him in the way and form that we first met. He suddenly sweeps me into an embrace exactly like a human hug, multiplied a thousand times by the energy of his Unconditional Love.

"Come, Michael, let's adjourn to the wide, open spaces."
When he lets go of me, we are in a forest.

I gaze around, spellbound. Surrounding us are the lar-
gest trees that I have ever seen. The biggest trees in our
few remaining areas of untouched forest would be dwarfed
by these. They are colossal! I recognize none of them.
There is an aura of ultimate perfection in this forest, of
some incredible synthesis between humanity and Nature.

"Make contact with a tree," the Shepherd suggests, as
though answering all my unspoken questions.

Drift-walking over to a tree whose lower branches sweep
the pungent soil with fingers of soft, pale green leaves, I
sit on a convenient and inviting branch. Within moments,
I feel an induced inner relaxation, and I let go of all my
many questions. With no sense of movement, my focus
is hovering just above the forest, a vast expanse of trees
stretching out below me. In some areas the sun shines
strongly into the forest, while in other parts of the forest
it is raining. As far as I can see and perceive, there is an
ocean of green foliage. Birds of many varieties fly in and
among the trees, their calls forming a background orches-
tra of muted sound. Butterflies flit and flutter among the
flowers, while bees drone in a monotone hum as they
search for nectar. Small animals scramble here and there,
or nimbly leap, but, oddly, there are none that I recognize.

I feel a powerful sense of belonging, as though I have
lived here, yet it does not feel familiar. Slowly, my focus
moves along the top of the forest, probing into the upper
realms of this natural wonderland. I feel as if I am being passed along from one tree to another, as though my

psyche is within their awareness and care. With this realization, I am suddenly aware of the consciousness of the
trees, and we are in communication.

"Relax, Light One, and flow with life. Before all things,
trust. Trust Self. Seek without searching, enquire without
questions, see beyond looking. Always follow your heart."

As the clear words fade from within my consciousness,
I am aware of Nature spirits all around me. As though my
vision has just cleared, I perceive that the forest is alive
with the Beings of Nature, from vast ethereal Beings that
seem to contain a whole tree to the very tiniest Beings possible. It reminds me of the realm of the Pillar of Green
Light. I realize that the people of this reality work within
the cooperation and influence of that mystic kingdom.

As my perception fades, I become aware that I am sitting on the low branch. Getting off, with care and respect
for the tree, I place my hand upon it reverently. I am not
sure why the Spirit of the Tree has imparted this particular message with such absolute clarity and impact, but I
feel a deep gratitude. "Thank you," I whisper.

Under the Shepherd's guidance, we drift like thistle seed
among the splendid trees. "In our reality frame this would
be exploited and ruined," I say. "We call it development
and progress. Apart from the wonder and beauty of the
forest simply being here, do the people of this frame use
it in any way?"

Smiling, the Shepherd changes our direction, and within
moments I see again the familiar, multicolored band of
energy. More rainbowlike than ever, it sweeps from beneath the trees to encircle some of them, then up, up, to

the canopy far above, only to come sweeping down again. Winding its way through the trees like a never-ending, iridescent tube of light, it is as much a part of the forest as it is of the city. With no solidity, no support, and without intruding, it belongs. Birds fly through it, animals ignore it, and flowers blossom within it as a breeze sweeps various outstretched branches into it.

With the Shepherd, I drift into the energy band. "Let's take our time," I ask. "I want to experience this rather than our instant arrival somewhere else."

There is nothing that I can possibly compare it to in our twentieth-century reality. At the speed of a fast run, we are swept through the forest as though we are flying/ standing. Thrillingly, we sweep up, up, then down and around, transported by an energy band that is designed to give those whom it transports a real experience of the living forest. "I suppose that this is the only transport needed in this reality," I murmur, mesmerized by the forest.

"Actually, no. This system serves a particular purpose, linking all the cities and visiting many major areas of commerce, natural wonder, and wilderness. There is a network like this over the whole planet, but people also have their own independent means of travel."

"Not cars!"

The Shepherd laughs. "Just wait and see."

Somewhere near the edge of the forest, we alight from the energy/transporter, drifting in a fast walk toward wide open spaces.

"How about a farm? I saw one in that other reality; may I see its comparison here?"

"That is exactly where we are heading," the Shepherd replies. "I can assure you that this will be more to your liking."

As we quite rapidly approach a cluster of domes, a large, completely transparent bubble floats silently and swiftly over us. Astonishingly, a person stands within it. With a sudden acceleration, it swoops down toward the domes, stopping not far from us. The occupant simply steps out of the bubble, moving through the sides as we would walk through a film of water. There are no controls or instrumentation to be seen in the conveyance. Even though it is far more potent, it looks just like a large, empty bubble.

"Wouldn't I like one of those!" I exclaim.

"That is a personal transporter," the Shepherd tells me. "Everybody over the age of six has one. The vehicle is attuned to its owner, responding to thought commands. It also—"

"Is it biological, alive?" I interject.

Frowning reprovingly, the Shepherd continues. "No, it is not biological. It is composed of harnessed electromagnetic energy; this is attuned with the energy field of its owner."

"Can it only transport the owner, or can anyone drive it, like a car?"

"A few are personally attuned only; most are programmed to accept anyone. However, each person has to attune with the vehicle before being transported."

"What! Like meditate before a journey? That's not much good if you're in a hurry!"

The Shepherd stares imploringly heavenward. "It takes

but mere seconds, Michael. This is not a backward or ar-
chaic frame of reality; this is a peak of spiritual focus and
intelligence. As in that other frame of reality, you are seeing but a tiny fraction of all that is here."

A deeply submerged knot of pure, undiluted inadequacy
suddenly forces its way out of me. "I know that," I say in
a shaky voice, but I don't know what I'm supposed to do
with it." I gulp. "I hear you tell me that I have to share
this, then I learn that I will forget practically all of it. I'm
lost, overwhelmed. I . . . why me?"

The Shepherd stares at me, his face registering enormous
compassion. Nodding, he says, "I understand. You see yourself as so little, so inadequate, while I see you as a Being
of Light, human, and powerfully adequate. Who of us is
the wiser? Who has the greater insight, the greater Truth?"

I can only stare back at him, speechless, threatened by
the sheer volume and magnitude of my experience.

"Michael, it was you who chose to enter this mystical
realm. You were not chosen by others. Nothing has been
imposed. You made this choice to assist in your Awakening. If you remain in the human dream, asleep, and everything that you have experienced is forgotten and lost, that
is not wrong or bad. It is all within the human consciousness, as is *all* the experience of *all* people. However, you
have chosen to Awaken in this incarnation, and this mystical adventure is an initiation, a beginning. And it is more,
for this experience of a timeless realm is not yours alone.
I repeat, in consciousness, it is shared with all humanity,
no matter how unaware other people may be of this. Nor
does it matter by how many it is rejected; *All is One.*

"Only if you Awaken will this be remembered as a happening experience. In other words, your memory will hold it in the past, but your reality will hold it in the moment. You will be able to accommodate this, and you will present the whole experience as a book for those of humanity who choose to share it. So powerfully will it be your ongoing experience of the moment that you will even write it in the more difficult style of the present tense, not knowing why it is so important that you do so until you are nearing the end.

"So relax. The Spirit of the Forest gave you the advice that you will most need. Before all things, trust your Self. Know that you are adequate — all humanity is adequate — and be gentle with yourself. Focus on all that you *are*, on your potential, your capabilities, your capacity. Ignore what you think you are not. Accept yourself the way you are. Trust yourself in all things at all times."

As I listen to the Shepherd on an inner telepathic level, I feel that each word is a vehicle for Love. I feel cocooned and nurtured in such a Lightness of Love that it breaks through my negating inadequacy like the bright sun through dark clouds. Hugging the Shepherd — Light to Light — I have no words, nor are they needed.

For a few timeless moments, I compose myself, then, in accord with the Shepherd, we drift over to the dome buildings. They are not very big, considerably smaller than an average house, and they look lightweight and flimsy.

The Shepherd grins at me. "Flimsy, they ain't," he says with exaggerated humor. "They would be impervious to your very worst tornadoes."

234

The passenger from the bubble appears not to have noticed us, for there is no sign of anyone around. We walk into the nearest dome, and I stare in surprise. It is empty.

"It's empty," I say, brilliant at stating the obvious.

Laughing, the Shepherd explains. "These domes are not farmyard buildings or barns the way you expected. They are force fields, designed to be enlarged to cover whole fields. Although these people have the technology and mental capacity to control the weather, they choose not to. They accept that the weather and the balance of Nature are so intrinsically interconnected that any interference would be detrimental to the Whole. What appears to you as a flimsy dome is really a collapsed field of force that can be expanded to cover hundreds of acres—in your measurement—of land. In this way the farmers control the ecology of an area and what they are growing without affecting any other areas of Nature."

"I suppose they are basically used in winter?"

"Mostly, also in other times of inclement weather. Each force field is programmed for what is needed. They are able to control temperature, rainfall, and several other factors, producing the required climatic conditions."

"So where does the farmer and his or her family live?"

"Unlike in your time/frame, they seldom live on the farm. Land is not owned; it belongs to everyone and is used for the welfare of all—human and Nature. The farming families live in villages, using their transporters to travel to the crops. This reality is very different from anything you are used to. Animals are not farmed. Cows are not kept for milk, nor sheep for wool, and there are no livestock for meat. Also, there are no pets. Birds and animals are free, companions only by choice."

"Do they ever choose to be pets, I mean, companions?"

"Frequently, but always for a focused higher purpose."

"Such as?"

"Humans and animals become companions when it is in the interests of both to learn from each other. Generally, such a bond is for the life term of the animal, although short-term bonding also occurs."

I stare at the Shepherd as a hundred more questions fight to be first. Holding up both hands, he hastens to speak. "Let go of your questions. The more you ask, the more you want to know. As in the previous frame, you are here to experience just the flavor and energy of this reality. It is far more different here than you can really comprehend—simpler, yet, at the same time, much more complex. There are no police, no armies, no greed, no crime. Everything that you need is here in abundance. Imagine what that implies. These people live in the moment, spiritually focused, learning to expand their consciousness, develop their intelligence, and increase their wisdom. They do this through their interaction with one another, and as students of the Spirit of Nature. They also learn from other Beings."

"You mean visitors from the stars?"

"That's a dramatic way to state it, but accurate."

"I take it that the Gray Ones are not welcome here."

The Shepherd chuckles. "They could not be here. The energy of aware and focused Love is anathema to them."

"Do any of the Beings I have met in this timeless realm come here?"

"Question time again?"

"How else can I know?"

"My answers are not your knowing; they are information, and information is not the experience of knowing. In fact, information can easily become a detour around knowing."

His energy has become brisk. "We will visit one of the crop fields in this reality, so you can experience it, and then we must return. You are beginning to wobble."

"Wobble? Me!"

I can feel the Shepherd's humor. "You are approaching the limit of your ability to stay within a metaphysical focus. You have done remarkably well."

I am aware of feeling vaguely light-headed, but I have no idea that my time is running out. "How ironic to run out of time in a timeless realm," I quip. I realize that it's the physical me who is feeling fatigued, and that, of course, affects the light-body me.

Without any awareness of drift or movement, we are suddenly in a large field of grain. What I am seeing is quite astounding. A house-sized bubble is floating over the field, while a stream of grain flows from the heads of the plants directly into the bubble. It fills quite rapidly, yet the bubble seems as light and buoyant as ever.

"That's impossible," I say.

"It is all made possible by a superconductive field of energy," the Shepherd explains. "However, I want you to empathize with the grain. Attune with it; feel the energies involved."

Although I have no idea what a superconductive field

of energy is, I am able to feel a powerful sense of release and fulfillment—a "mission accomplished" feeling—as the grain flows into the bubble. I "feel" the cooperaton between the plants and the people involved, even though there is no one here to supervise.

As I watch, the bubble fills, and with a brief flicker, it accelerates out of sight in less than a microsecond. Immediately, with no lessening of the flow and without losing any grain, another large bubble is there receiving it.

"Put simply, the people of this reality are masters at the creation and use of force fields. Grain forms the basis of many of their foods, along with a diversity of fruit and vegetables that would leave you gasping. Suffice it to say that the number of fruit and vegetable species in regular use is in the thousands," the Shepherd says.

Watching the grain being harvested is like being a witness to magic. It is inconceivable by my standards. As though caught in cyclonic yet gentle force, the swirling ripple where the grain is leaving the plant is completely soundless, adding a surreal quality to this impossible scene.

Suddenly, I am very aware of my wobble! I feel increasingly light-headed, with the overtone of an enormous fatigue slowly closing in on me. The Shepherd knows this, and although I keep expecting us to return to his craft, he hesitates.

Without warning, a bubble containing three people comes sweeping over the grain crop to hover close by us. Staring hard at them, I gasp. Two are tan-skinned human adults, but the other Being, although humanoid, is fine-boned and very slender, with a large hairless head and startling blue skin. For a moment our eyes meet, and I sense an inner recognition. I feel a love for this Being that is so powerful and unexpected, it hurts. In the brief moment our eyes meet, I feel a promise from the Blue Being that I cannot put into words — a promise I cannot define.

Even as I stare longingly back, everything around me blurs, and with no sense of movement or displacement, we are back in the Shepherd's craft.

I realize that the Shepherd deliberately delayed so that I could meet the Blue Being. I smile into the Shepherd's eyes. "Thank you. With all that I am, thank you." Despite the Mystery — or maybe because of it — I have no questions.

10
And So It Begins

The higher, finer, vibration of Love
sweeping the planet will bring new change.
For some, this will herald the choice of Awakening;
for others, it will quicken the awakening of choice.

My fatigue is developing into a throbbing ache, tugging my awareness back to the physical frailty that is ultimately in control. Despite this, I want more. I gaze at the long row of panels that seem to fade endlessly into the distance of the bi-spatial room, and, like a drunkard, I want more.

Walking to the next panel, I gaze into a scene of snow and ice. I look at the Shepherd inquiringly. "Another reality frame?" I ask.

"An ice age," he replies. "Many of the people of your present reality will experience this, for it is within their consciousness that the Earth must be healed in such a way, and humanity punished."

"Nature doesn't punish," I protest.

"This is true; there is no retribution in Nature. Nature is *balance*, physically demonstrating the principle of cause and effect. However, those who are attached to the concept of environmental injustice and the need for punishment will experience an ice-age reality. Never forget, we each create our own reality. This is the prime Truth that holds us all within its creative framework."

With the intent of hastening to another panel, I attempt to walk to the next in line, but my light body will not respond. I try to struggle, but even this is denied me. I relax, and I am easily able to follow the Shepherd as we walk to the door and out of the room.

"You have seen and experienced enough, Michael, more than enough. Is it a genuine hunger for Truth, or is it a greed that wants more?"

Chastened, I willingly follow the Shepherd. The last time I walked the corridor, it seemed unfathomably long, but as I follow the Shepherd it leads us straight into the room where I first entered the craft. The same silvery brightness is apparent, although it no longer dazzles me.

The Shepherd gestures to a blank wall, transforming it instantly into a large, clear window. I have the impression that we are flying, and that far beneath us I can see the planet Earth. What confuses me is the incredible aura of white Light that glows like a vast nimbus around the planet. So powerful is the aura I can scarcely see through it to the physical Earth.

"Is that really Earth?" I whisper in awe.

"It certainly is," the Shepherd replies.

"But . . . but why don't I see it in the same way that our astronauts do? I'm above it. Our space photographs show it to be a brilliant blue and green, with city lights visible from far out."

"Earth is indeed a beautiful gem, however you view it Your astronauts view it from a physical reality, and

243

naturally, the photographs reflect this. We are not physically traveling in space, looking down onto Earth; we are unfolding through frames of reality, viewing Earth from a metaphysical aspect."

"Oh! I didn't know that Earth, or any planet, could have an aura, let alone have one as magnificent as this."

"Is it conceivable that a planet that is considered as home by Beings of Light—humanity—could be any less of a Light Being itself? The planet that humanity is presently learning its lessons on also has a developing consciousness. The destinies of humanity and Earth are intrinsically bound at this stage of growth. That which uplifts and elevates humanity does the same for Earth; equally, those actions that defile Nature, and therefore the Earth, are detrimental to humanity."

I gaze at the vast aura of Light, humbled. As I feast my soul on its beauty, I notice a clear, shimmering vibration sparkling with brilliant flecks of light as it drifts from the heavens over the face of the Earth. "What is that?"

The Shepherd smiles, his Love radiant. "Michael, in the years to come, you will witness a birth. For many ages, a spiritual wisdom has been growing within humanity, and its birthing is imminent. It will be the selective birthing of those who, for many incarnations, have focused on their spiritual growth and insight. *All* birth is choice, *always*."

"How does this relate to the sparkling light that I can see? And where do I fit in all this?"

If there is anything that is infinite, it must be the patience of the Shepherd. He smiles at me, not just tolerantly, but with his all-embracing Love.

Stepping close to me, he passes his hand slowly across my eyes. I gasp. In some incredible way, I can see over all the Earth at the same time. I see/perceive that the sparkling vibration of light is permeating every living thing on the planet. All minerals and all the various trace elements, every plant, from the great trees to the lichen, each and every insect, bird, and animal, every human Being— all are suffused and permeated by this new, more potent vibration of Light. Even the air, water, fire, and the body of Earth itself.

"Nature is responding to this higher, finer vibration of Love," the Shepherd explains. "There is no choice in this for Nature, for Nature always aligns with the natural order of life. Humanity, however, must choose to respond to this new frequency of Love. This is the choice of free will; it means that to be Free, your 'will' must be aligned with Love. For some, this will herald the choice of Awakening; for others, it will quicken the awakening of choice."

"I take it that the vibration I can see now is not visible on a physical level?"

"It is only spiritually visible. Open the eyes of the soul, and it will dazzle you."

"So what happens to me now?" I ask lamely. "Do I return to the struggle?"

The Shepherd's smile is pure love. "That, too, is your choice. You may return to the struggle, as you call it, or you can use your 'will' and return to a willing surrender. I do not pretend that this is easy. For most, there will be chaos, conflict, and fear, and this will reflect the lack of choice. Choose Love; surrender to Self."

I sigh deeply. Like most of humanity, I am tightly bound by my habitual conditioning. I desperately want to choose Love rather than fear, and acceptance rather than struggle and denial, but I don't know how.

"My struggle will be in letting go of fear and trying to choose Love. It is so difficult," I tell the Shepherd.

"You have just defined the basis of all human conflict. I repeat, trust Self—and surrender to who you are. The vibration you see will assist you. Attune to your highest ideals and principles, and the vibration of Love will take you into higher levels of Self."

"And if . . . when . . . I Awaken, I must share this experience of mine with other people?"

"That, too, you have chosen."

"Is there one single factor of unity in all this—just one Truth or Reality I can hold onto when I feel that I am drowning in the morass of everyday life?"

Reaching out, the Shepherd places a glowing hand onto my shoulder. "Michael, I can only reiterate what I have already said, and what every experience in this timeless realm has been teaching you: *All Life is the diversity of One.* This is the Great Truth that all humanity is learning. You are each God-in-the-making. Even for potential Gods, to create only with infinite Love and wisdom is a concept until it has become realized. To get past this concept, you who are God-in-the-making are obliged to live your own creation. This reveals another prime truth: *You each create your own reality.* If you create separation, then your reality will give birth to fear, and you will live fearfully, experiencing its wide range of consequences. If you create judgment, then you will live with being judged. All negativity you express toward other people will always reflect back into your own life. It has been most aptly said, 'What you sow, you must reap.' Now is the time to sow Love, reaping the rich and abundant harvest of soul fulfillment."

Listening, I realize that despite having this knowledge, I will still be faced with the challenge of *living* it.

The Shepherd continues. "Collectively, humanity slumbers; Awakening is an individual process. As each new person shatters the deception of separation, individually knowing Oneness as a reality, the Light aura of Earth will grow ever greater, until, eventually, it will become a beacon of triumph throughout the whole multiverse.

"For you, Michael, this timeless realm is coming to an end. You have both a focus and a purpose in Awakening. As you and others like you emerge from the dream, knowing and experiencing the Great Truth of life, by this action you will renew the Earth. Love will be the Earth's outpouring."

There is no sensation of movement, no swooping down to Earth in the Shepherd's craft, yet as I stand at the window watching the sparkling vibration that sweeps like glittering dust over all the land, I suddenly see my loved and familiar river.

Turning to the Shepherd, I stare at him helplessly. I want to ask a thousand questions. I want to cry. I want him to remain in my life. I want . . . . I want. . . . Like a fish, my mouth opens and closes silently, while the nimbus of Light that surrounds the Shepherd grows ever stronger, reaching out until I am embraced and held within it. For long moments, I feel the power of his Love, and within that Love I hear again the Song—the Song of Oneness.

How long I remain cocooned in the Shepherd's aura, I have no idea, but when I again become aware, I am standing, bewildered, on the riverbank.

With a sadness that threatens to overwhelm me, I gaze up into the early morning sky, searching for the Golden Globe, but I stand alone. Even the river is normal. There is nothing even to suggest that the river had flowed steeply and outrageously uphill—no evidence that in this place I entered a timeless realm of pure wonder.

The golden dawn remains the same, with the sun in the same position it was earlier. As I stare at the sun, I get a momentary impression of some vast awareness, as though I am being watched by some colossal cosmic eye. On impulse, I smile and wink at the sun.

I turn away, my mind awhirl. Am I asleep or awake? The answer to this is clear, for I am aware of waves of fatigue emanating from my physical body, slumped in my bed. I still have the same body of light with which I began this strange adventure, but now I am being strongly drawn toward my physical body.

Floating in a fast walk across the field, I am powerless to deny the physical pull. I am conscious that I am changed. It would be impossible to go through all that I have experienced and not be! I know that I have been through some wondrous initiation, and I realize that rather than coming to an end, it is really all about to begin.

Within my psyche, I feel the Light that I have experienced, and I know that the Song will never leave me. I may well forget how to listen, and I probably will no longer be able to hear it, but the Song cannot be diminished. No matter what it takes, or how long, I will learn to open my heart and once again hear the Song.

I had no awareness of finishing my journey across the field, or even of entering our house. All I know is that, suddenly, I was aware of sitting slumped in bed, my pen in hand as I finished my frenzied writing. I held the pad before me, gaping at the pages of scrawled words.

The exhaustion that I now felt was unlike any tiredness I had ever experienced. I felt a strange, vast, yet fading elation mixed with an utter weariness that seemed to come from some inner place, sweeping through me as wave after wave of unremitting fatigue.

Glancing at the illuminated dial, I saw that it was five o'clock. My God! Three hours had gone by. What happened to me? The first light of early morning was just beginning to peep through the chinks around our bedroom curtain as, in awe, I began to recollect all that had happened. As I lay there, trying to remember, the enormity of it frightened me.

I glanced at Treenie, peacefully sleeping. Would she remember her part in all this, or would it be forgotten in the aggravating way of dreams? I decided to wake her and find out, and then tell her all about my ensuing adventures. I was full to the brim, I had so much I wanted to tell her. At the very top of the list, I wanted to tell her of my vow to Awaken. Had I made such a vow? I must have been mad! I dropped the pen and pad to the floor and lay back for a few moments to relax. I wanted to search for the right words to make it all sound feasible, or credible; instead, exhausted, I fell asleep!

Epilogue

Unfortunately, my everyday reality proved the Shepherd to be right. My unwanted resistance to inner change and my unwanted attachment to all that is so-called normal —our consensus reality—was very strong. A few years of traumatic inner conflict tore me apart before I finally accepted the timeless reality of that other realm. As anticipated, the everyday me was so fearful of being different that I tried to deny my own experience, but I had it documented in my own handwriting. Or at least, about ten percent of it! More than anything else, the stark confrontation of my own written account denied me any chance of dismissal. My metaphysical adventure confronted me more than anything I had ever faced. Beings I had not even dreamed of had guided me, ignited me, opened me, nurtured me, and challenged me.

I was faced with a twofold task. I had to Awaken to the Truth of Self, and become open to the mystical realm of Nature. The fact that I was a person of low self-esteem made it all the more difficult. My other books— *Talking With Nature* and *Journey Into Nature*—explain what happened as

I gradually went through the spiritual transition that is unique to humanity. In *Journey Into Oneness*, I attempt to share some fraction of my metaphysical experiences within a greater holistic reality.

The experience I have documented in this book took place in 1977. The years that followed were not easy. My path was a strange duality. One aspect was of pain, suffering, and all the anxiety that comes with oceans of self-doubt, while the other was a metaphysical journey into a mystical Nature. However, despite the trauma, I persisted. I went through my Awakening in 1986. My "do or die" vow came very close to ending my physical life. In fact, for who *I am* to become my reality, my identity self did, indeed, die. But, I know who I Am. I know also that you, reading this, can know your own truth of Self.

More than anything, you will need commitment. You will need to focus on *your* Awakening, and follow the dictates of *your* heart. Your mind will scream at you, confusing you, but you will need the courage to follow that tiny whisper from the heart. Trust yourself. Do it with Love. Having traveled on the path of pain, I don't recommend it. Love is the natural way—loving yourself. Practice by being gentle with yourself, even while you are being relentless. Learn to be open to the miraculous; it makes the process so much easier! Never forget that your reality, your truth, is *far, far, far* greater than your knowledge of it. You are a metaphysical, multidimensional Being of Light, and you will need to expand in your consciousness to accept and experience this—your divinity.

Epilogue

Life will provide your teachers in perfect timing. Some of them you will welcome; others you may try to reject. My teachers were Nature and people. Nature was welcome; people were not. Even though I had to enter the mystical realms of Nature for much of my Self-discovery, it was my daily contact with people that enforced the lessons I learned. It was easy to be peaceful with Nature, but if I did not feel that same peace when interacting with other people, then my peace was no more than another deceit, another illusion.

Never try to copy other people. Be true to yourself. My series of four books relating to Nature and Self tell of my metaphysical journey into, and through, my Awakening. This is my reality; it may not be yours. I get a lot of mail from people on a similar path, but, equally, I get as much mail from people who are not. Many people would like to have mystical encounters like mine, but none of them want the gut-wrenching uncertainty, or the heart-rending isolation and loneliness, that I used to experience afterward. None of them ask for the devastating sense of loss that I used to feel when I returned to a normal reality. Without Treenie, I would have been lost to despair. There were times when I experienced such mystical beauty that I became oversensitized, and just living in the world was an ordeal. This was my path, a path of my choosing. You, also, have chosen your path, and it is to your path, and your Self, that you must be true. The simple fact is we are all magnificent Beings, seeking Self in the way that most pertains to us, right now. We are all unique, wonderfully different, each ot us having our own relevant experiences in our different realities.

In our individual uniqueness, we each have the ability to open ourselves to the greater, more expanded Reality of Self. The only way through our fear-based resistance and its accompanying trauma is to accept our own reality, no matter how different it may be. That's easier said than done. Most sensitive people fear being different. I am aware that being different caused many of us to endure torture and death in previous lives, and the imprint of this trauma is still within our consciousness. We feel safer now if we accept a consensus reality. However, despite the obvious need to provide for our everyday welfare, we are not on this planet merely to be safe or comfortable or even secure; we are here to open ourselves to a Greater Truth, a Greater Reality.

We are here to expand in our awareness and grow in consciousness. We are here to unfold and flower, and to share the fragrance of our uniqueness with other people. Each one of us is here to experience the Truth of Self, of who I Am. After all the intellectual ideas and concepts have been discussed, after all the words have been written and spoken, and after all the personal growth workshops have been attended, finally we still have to *accept* ourselves the way we are—even *love* ourselves— and *live* our own reality. We can do this in a remarkably simple way, by choosing the path of honor. All we have to do is *honor* ourselves in our daily thoughts, in our spoken words, and in our everyday actions. Before all things, as we live to honor Self, we Awaken to our Truth.

About the Author

Michael J. Roads was born in England, and from the time he was a child delving into the mysteries of a hidden, silent Nature, he has spent his life as an outdoorsman. His background is based in farming, and after marrying Treenie, they emigrated to Australia. During a decade of farming on the island state of Tasmania, Michael went through profound changes, gradually becoming attuned to the Spirit of the Land. This change was to take him away from farming and into a search for Self. Difficult years were to follow, but the inner search was unrelenting. To be free and to know Self was all that had meaning.

During this time, Michael and Treenie experienced community life, followed by a few years of Michael working as an organic farming consultant. Daily he focused on empowering his conscious, aware, spiritual connection with Nature. He learned to cross the membrane separating the material (physical) from the intangible (metaphysical). Writing about this experience became his creative outlet.

Michael's life now consists of writing, playing, and giving Retreats. With Treenie, he conducts five-day Retreats in

Australia, the United States, the United Kingdom, South Africa, and Europe. He asks only that all participants be committed!

He is a brilliant speaker. He is also "Awake." He speaks his truth clearly, without dogma or bias. He is funny, inspiring, and direct. He lives his truth. Above all, however, he is simple. He teaches no techniques, but, in his own words, "I teach people to practice a Greater Reality, and to keep practicing until the Greater Reality overwhelms the illusion."

He has a dislike of organizations, and thus he belongs to none, nor will he allow any to form around him. He and Treenie are free spirits. They are, however, open to correspondence.

The Roadsway Tapes

These cassettes were recorded during some of Michael's talks and seminars, engendering all the impromptu interaction that a live audience elicits. Although the titles may remain the same—or even be changed!—these tapes are continually being updated; thus, the spoken content will vary over a period of time.

M1	The Spirit of Nature	$U.S.16.00
M2	It's Time to Wake Up	$U.S.16.00
M4	Principles for Living	$U.S.16.00
M5	Awareness in Organic Culture	$U.S.16.00
T1	Treenie's Story (by Treenie)	$U.S.16.00
M15	Oneness of All Life	$U.S.16.00
M16	Taking Back Your Power (two tapes)	$U.S.30.00

M13 Awakening to Self (four tapes) $U.S.55.00
M14 Oneness With Nature (six tapes) $U.S.75.00

The price of the cassettes includes postage and packing.

"A Timeless Realm" — The Cassette

Written by Michael, "A Timeless Realm" is the account of one of his mystical journeys into a metaphysical reality. Deeply evocative, "A Timeless Realm" is spoken by Treenie, while the musical genius of Mars Lazar (*Olympus* and *The Eleventh Hour*) is breathtaking. Hauntingly beautiful, "A Timeless Realm" is totally unique.

The cost, including postage and packing, is $U.S.23.00.

Organic Gardening Book

Michael is also the well-known author of a book on organic gardening: *The Natural Magic of Mulch*. Published in Australia, *The Natural Magic of Mulch* is an acclaimed book on the philosophical and practical applications of mulching and no-dig gardening. It covers cold, temperate, and subtropical climates.

The cost, including postage and packing, is $U.S.25.00.

For correspondence and Retreat Workshop information, any of the tapes, or the mulch book, please write to:

Michael and Treenie Roads
P.O. Box 778
Nambour, QLD, 4560
Australia